The History of Kalmykia:
From Ancient Times
to Kirsan Ilyumzhinov and Aleksey Orlov

The History of Kalmykia:
From Ancient Times to Kirsan Ilyumzhinov and Aleksey Orlov

Justin Corfield

GENTEXT PUBLICATIONS
2015

Gentext Publications
An imprint of Corfield and Company

This edition first published in Australia, 2015
by Gentext Publications
59 Smeaton Close, Lara, Victoria, 3212, Australia

National Library of Australia
Cataloguing-in-publication data

Creator: Corfield, Justin J., author.

Title: The history of Kalmykia : from ancient times to
Kirsan Ilyumzhinov and Aleksey Orlov / Justin Corfield.

ISBN: 9781876586294 (hardback)

Notes: Includes index.

Subjects: Iliumzhinov, Kirsan, 1962-
        Orlov, Alekseĭ M. (Alekseĭ Mikhaĭlovich) 1961-
        World Chess Federation--History.
        Presidents--Russia (Federation)--Kalmykiĭa--Biography
        Chess players--Biography
        Kalmykiĭa (Russia)--History.

Dewey Number: 947.48004942

Contents

Introduction

Located north of the Caucasus Mountains, on the west coast of the Caspian Sea, since the 1990s, Kalmykia has occasionally in the world news either on account of an important chess match, or some aspect of the life of its president, Kirsan Ilyumzhinov, who is also president of the International Chess Federation (FIDE). There have only been a small number of books in English on Kalmyk history, and also a number which cover aspects of the career of Kirsan Ilyumzhinov. However this is the first in English to combine the two, and try to explain the history of Kalmykia and the role of Kirsan Ilyumzhinov in the emergence of Kalmykia after the end of Communism, and the further development of the country under its current president, Aleksey Orlov.

In April 2009, at the invitation of President Kirsan Ilyumzhinov and his Minister of Education Badma Salayev, I led a school chess team on the first western school trip to Kalmykia, and during our time in the Republic of Kalmykia we were so warmly welcomed by both President Kirsan Ilyumzhinov himself, and also so many people in Kalmykia. We met President Ilyumzhinov on six occasions, participated in two chess tournaments, and against school teams in Elista, and also travelled throughout the countryside, meeting people in remote towns and hamlets and farms, getting a deep insight into the republic and the obvious problems which have faced it before and also since the collapse of Communism.

It is easy to criticise any part of the world, and sadly some of the books, magazine articles or television programs which mention Kalmykia have jumped at the opportunity to do so. There are social problems, and there is poverty and underdevelopment. But Kalmykia is not unique in any of these areas. In fact there are few countries in the world which do not have one, or the other, or both. After so many centuries of service to the Russian state, it was during much of the twentieth century that the Kalmyk people have been so badly persecuted. Their deportation to Siberia for thirteen years resulted in a national trauma, as it has in other groups similarly treated by Josef Stalin. But rather than react with hatred, what I found in Kalmykia was an inspiring example of multicultural harmony. It is a place where Buddhists, Christians and Muslims coexist happily. And all this is not that far from Chechnya and Georgia

Kalmucke.   Physiognomie der Kalmucken.   Kalmückin.

Kalmucken aus dem Volke.   Priester der Kalmucken u. Fürstin.

Kampfspiele der Kalmücken.

Lager der Kalmücken

Japan

Ansicht von Miako.

Das Innere eines kalmückischen Zeltes.

X

where so many lives and so much infrastructure was destroyed in fighting in recent years which has produced few, if any, real victors.

Kirsan Ilyumzhinov has led a new nationalist revival in Kalmykia, but one that has championed the Kalmyk identity and also its close identification with the Russian state. He has combined this with the promotion of chess which has made Elista, the capital of Kalmykia, for a period, the undoubted centre of world chess, and it was for this reason that we accepted his invitation to travel from Australia to Kalmykia in 2009.

The idea was partially that of one of my students. It was a hot December afternoon in 2007 when our school chess club was gathering to play some games. One of the boys, Gregory Toth, then thirteen, was reading the school bulletin about a cricket tour and he suggested that our school should organise a chess tour. With Russia as the homeland of so many chess players, we decided that this had to be the destination, and it was my father who reminded me that many years earlier we had watched a television news bulletin about the construction of Chess City in Kalmykia.

There were only a few largely inconsequential books on Kalmykia written at that time. Kirsan Ilyumzhinov had said to Ed Vuillamy of *The Guardian*, 'What I say to these critics is this: Come to Kalmykia! Come to Elista and see! You will find simple people here, living in order and in peace while all around there is war and terrorism.' After we wrote to President Ilyumzhinov, he invited us to come to Kalmykia and see the place for ourselves and make up our own minds. This we decided to do.

Just before our visit, the intrepid Australian traveller Tim Cope had been through Kamlykia in his journey from Mongolia to Hungary. It was one of the places he visted about which he spoke most affectionately. However his account of his time there was published after our travels.

Our school's first trip to Elista was delayed for six months owing to the war in Georgia, but in April 2009 I led a group of ten – including Greg, by then aged fifteen. We arrived on Kirsan Ilyumzhinov's birthday and we headed straight from the airport to his office. He hosted us for an unforgettable week in Kalmykia in which the boys played chess and we also visited most parts of the Republic. Two years later another intrepid group of twelve of us – again including Greg – were back in Elisa. This book is one of the results of these two trips, and a subsequent visit to Elista.

Many accounts of Kalmykia in the press and on the internet claim the republic has been the centre of a massive personality cult focused by President Ilyumzhinov on himself. Books by otherwise reputable publishers claim that Kalmykia is a police state and people live in fear under the eyes of some watchful Orwellian 'Big Brother'. Internet blog sites carry anonymous criticisms of the place by people who have clearly never been there, and the public perception of Kalmykia has been fanned by paranoia and misinformation.

On three visits, I saw no public posters of Kirsan Ilyumzhinov – but many of the Dalai Lama – and much to my disappointment I was unable to get a copy of his autobiography in Elista on the first two trips, although I was able to buy a copy of one of his books from a secondhand stall, and several by his father from a bookshop. There is no razor wire around Chess City. Locals can wander in and out of it freely, and many non-Chess events are also held there. People came up to us at Chess City, and while we were walking around Elista, and they greeted us and chatted to us amiably. We were on the television news almost every night, so they all knew who we were. In spite of press claims to the contrary, the opposition newspaper is openly sold in news stalls outside both the main hotels.

One of my abiding memories was of attending an Orthodox Easter service after which an old Russian lady greeted one of my colleagues and told him she was overjoyed to hear that we had travelled so far to see her city and hoped we enjoyed our time there and tell everybody about it. At Tsagan Aman we were told we were some of the first western visitors since World War II – a slight exaggeration as a British reporter had written about the town in *The Geographical Magazine* seven years earlier.

There are many people I must thank for making this work possible. First and foremost I must thank Greg Toth who helped suggest the idea, and my father who encouraged me in the planning of such a complicated itinerary. I must also thank Kirsan Ilyumzhinov who met with us eight times during our time in Elista, and to his father Nicholas Ilyumzhinov who helped provide me many details about his family's history, and to his brother Vyacheslav Ilyumzhinov whom we met briefly. President Alexsey Orlov who granted me a very long interview and spoke about his future plans for Kalmykia, and I am grateful for his help and encouragement. I must also thank Yelena Pokinanova and Angelica Bakanova Dambayeva, and Larisa, who made so many things possible, and, as did Ludmilla Ivanova, then minister of education (now prime minister).

Vice President Valery Boyaev was often on hand to help with arrangements, including driving me from the airport. And I must also thank Buyancha Galzanov, Victor Perkovsky, and Marina Plischenko of the Embassy of the Republic of Kalmykia to the President of the Russian Federation in Moscow, and many other officials. And of course Anna, Zayana, and Anna for looking after me on my last visit to Elista and for translating so much information for me.

In addition, this work also could not have been written without the authors who have already written about Kalmykia – both those who like me have come to love the place, and those who, for whatever reason, have been more hostile.

My final acknowledgements must be to my father who taught me how to play chess, and who encouraged me to go to Kalmykia in 2009. He read a very early draft of this book before his death, and I dedicate the book to his memory.

Justin Corfield

March 2015

1.
The Early History of the Kalmyks

It was about 3.30 am on 27 June 1709, and there was a crisp morning breeze blowing as the Swedish soldiers began to form up north of the town of Poltava in the Ukraine. The Swedish forces numbered only 24,000 and they were attacking the Russians who counted 52,000 regulars in fortified positions, reinforced by some 23,000 Russian irregular cavalry. However the Swedes were battle-hardened and most of them were veterans of previous battles which they had won in spite of these odds being stacked against them. However this time their leader, the impetuous and eccentric King Charles XII had been lain low by an injury to his foot incurred ten days earlier. Giving the command to two of his generals, he had made the decision that he had to attack so that his outnumbered soldiers would at least have the advantage of surprise. He probably would have ordered an attack anyway, but on the previous day he had just heard that a large force of Kalmyk cavalry was heading towards Poltava and he feared that their presence would give the Russians an even clearer advantage.

The Victory Memorial at Poltava
Photograph © Vladyslav Danilin / Fotolia.com

As the Swedes made their way slowly, quietly, and cautiously towards the Russian lines, most knew it was a battle crucial to their survival with their army trapped in the Ukraine. It was also a battle which, over the next seven hours would decide the fate of Eastern Europe for the next two centuries.

Some of the Kalmyk cavalry had arrived before the fighting began, and others arrived during the battle. But it was the fear of a large contingent of reinforcements that caused the Swedes to launch their ultimately abortive attack. Almost exactly one hundred years earlier, the Kalmyk lands had become a part of the Russian state, but the terror which was evoked by the Kalmyks was not from that alliance but from the time of the Mongol attack into Central Europe in 1241 when the Oirats (the ancestors of the Kalmyks) formed part of the massive Mongol invasion force. This fear of nomadic cavalry from the shores of the Caspian Sea was enough to force the hand of King Charles XII.

The Caspian Sea has long marked a part of the boundary between Europe and Asia. In ancient times, the trade routes, such as the famed Silk Road connecting China with the Roman Empire, went through Persia, running past the south of the Caspian Sea.

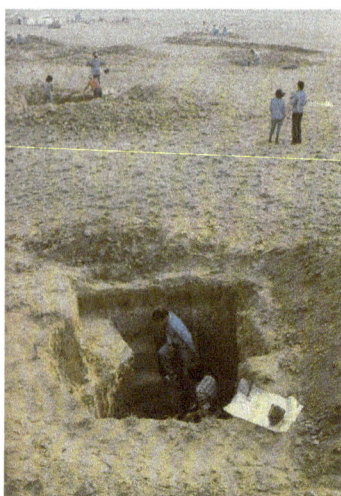

Archaeologists working in Kalmykia during the 1970s.

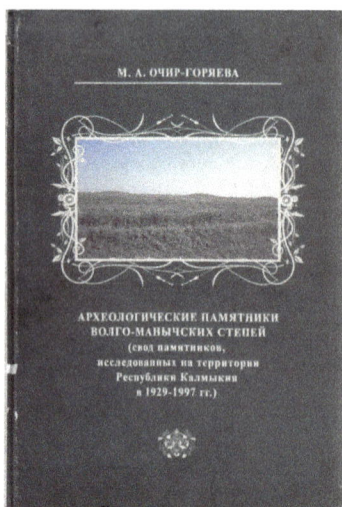

М. А. ОЧИР-ГОРЯЕВА

АРХЕОЛОГИЧЕСКИЕ ПАМЯТНИКИ
ВОЛГО-МАНЫЧСКИХ СТЕПЕЙ
(свод памятников,
исследованных на территории
Республики Калмыкия
в 1929-1997 гг.)

The Caucasus Mountains, on the northern border of the Persian Empire ensured that the region which became Kalmykia was generally bypassed by most of the early traders and travellers, and as a result little is known about that part of the world until medieval times.

Archaeologists who have worked in the territory of Kalmykia have found evidence of Neolithic settlements. For the most part these have consisted of burial mounds which contain bones and a few simple tools. In 1929, under the direction of Professor P. S. Rikov, archaeologists worked on thirteen sites in Kalymkia. In 1931-33, he carried out much more extensive work in Elista, and then worked on three other sites from 1933 to 1937. Unfortunately no Kalmyks were involved in these digs and with Rikov perishing in one of Stalin's prisons, there was no local expertise, and indeed because of the period of the Siberian exile, there was little interest in archaeological work until it started again in 1962 under Dr Shilov, and then under Professor I. V. Sinitsin, and continued by Professor U. E. Erdniev. Much of the work was in the form of 'rescue archaeology' with quick digs after remains had been uncovered during construction work. Gradually work was able to start on promising sites around the region. These excavations in recent years have yielded pots, candle-holders, and even a gold brooch, as well as a number of metal studs which were used to hold bridles and reins on their horses. It is believed that the landscape in those days might well be similar to that of the Steppes today – windswept plains with few trees. There was not much agricultural land, and the lack of pasture meant that the inhabitants were nomadic, lived in tents, and became strongly reliant on horses.

There are a number of reasons for the lack of trees in the Steppes. Certainly in some areas humans are responsible. But from about 600,000 B.C. until 370,000 B.C., herds of Steppe Mammoths (*Mammuthus trogontherii*) roamed the area and it has been suggested by some writers that these might have been responsible for ensuring that little woodland remained, in the same way as many naturalists believe that elephants are responsible for causing the Savanna landscapes in parts of Africa. The very hot summers and the cold winters meant that the people living there carved out a precarious existence.

The earliest surviving written account of the region is by the Greek writer Herodotus (c.484-425 B.C.), although he never went there. He wrote of the Scythians, a nomadic equestrian culture which originated in Central Asia and lived in the region through to the modern Ukraine. Herodotus wrote that before the Scythians, the Cimmerians lived north of the Caucasus Mountains occupying the lands covering the area from modern-day Kalmykia to the southern Ukraine. They flourished from the mid-eighth century to the early fourth century B.C., and also had maintained an Indo-European culture centred on the horse. Herodotus relied on information from others and some recent historians, quoting Assyrian sources, have argued that the Cimmerians did in fact lived on the south of the Caucasus Mountains, and that Herodotus was wrong. However Herodotus did demonstrate the accuracy of his sources as he maintained that the Caspian Sea was an inland sea; later classical writers such as Ptolemy claimed that it connected with an ocean to the north.

The World of Herodotus.

Whether or not the Cimmerians did live in present-day Kalmykia, it seems likely that the Scythians were not the first equestrian culture that flourished in the region. However they did dominate the region until Roman times when they began to merge with the Sarmatians, another group of equestrian nomadic pastoralists. The Scythians and the Sarmatians, as well as other peoples who lived in the Steppes, managed large herds of horses, cattle and later camels, moving around regularly to find new lands to graze their animals.

The Greek writer Strabo (d. c.24 A.D.), writing about the area occupied by the Scythians mentions the saiga antelope (*Saiga tatarica*) which he called the *kolos*, and described it as halfway between a ram and a deer, but able to drink through its nose.

By Roman times, what is now Kalmykia was controlled by the Sarmatians. Roman rule never reached into Kalmykia,

A saiga herd in the 1970s.

Saiga antelope, by Richard Lydekker.

3

Afgodsbeeld der Kalmukken.

A Kalmyk 'idol'.

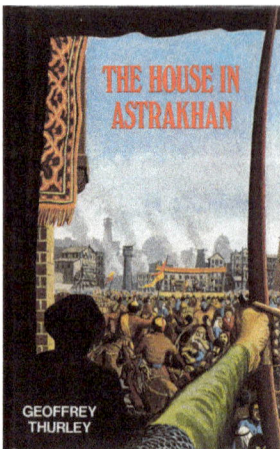

THE HOUSE IN ASTRAKHAN

GEOFFREY THURLEY

and written records on the Sarmatians are sparse. Except for classical scholars and war game enthusiasts, few people outside the region had heard of them until the film *King Arthur* (2004) bizarrely linked the legendary English king with a Roman cavalry officer who was given Sarmatian ancestry. There were certainly Sarmatians serving in the Roman cavalry, including some in Britain, but the connection made in the film certainly appears fanciful.

Although the Sarmatians were warlike, by the fourth century A.D., much of their land had been overrun by the Huns, yet another horse-oriented nomadic society, which swept through the region. The Hun route into Europe was north of present-day Kalmykia, and it seems likely that Sarmatian culture in Kalmykia might have survived for some centuries, especially as the power of the Huns waned after only eighty years. The rise of Islam did affect the region greatly with many of the people within the Caucasus Mountains embracing Islam. Traders would have also brought the religion to Kalmykia but it did not attract many converts amongst the locals.

From the seventh century, the Khazars emerged in control of the Caucasus and the southern Steppes. Their origin remains obscure but they may have been connected with the Uighurs from modern-day China, or were descendants of the Huns, or perhaps a combination of the two. Certainly their kingdom included people of a vast range of nationalities and religions, and the leaders converted to Judaism. They ran the empire for three centuries always facing possible war with the Christian Byzantines, and the Muslim Turks and Persians. Eventually the Khazar Empire also waned, and the lands which now form Kalmykia were controlled by the Sabirs, a Turkic tribe, and the Alans who descend from the Sarmatians. All these were still largely nomadic equestrian cultures, although the Khazars had established settlements such as Atil, Khazaran and Samandar.

It seems possible that during the period of the Crusaders, some intrepid European soldiers or traders might have visited the region although no accounts of their journeys are known to have survived. Geoffrey Thurley's novel *The House in Astrakhan* (1977) tells the story of a fictional journey of a Saxon, a Norman and a Scotsman – passing through the region, venturing to the city of Astrakhan in the thirteenth century. During that period the city was known as Xacitarxan, and is close to the site of the modern city. It was a major trading centre for many years but was attacked and sacked by the Mongol leader Tamerlane in 1395.

It was the arrival of the Mongols that was to change the entire region. In the early thirteenth century the Mongols had started to extend their rule westwards. Their origins lay in an equestrian nomadic culture not unlike those of the Scythians, Sarmatians and Huns. Coming from the plains of Mongolia, they were notorious for their ferocity in war, and they soon conquered a large empire preferring the Steppes where their cavalry had an advantage over any of their opponents. As with the previous equestrian societies, men were constantly involved in hunting and fighting. They were taught from a young age how to ride a horse, and use a bow. They all fought on horseback and engaged their enemies in battle when it suited them, and they retreated into the Steppes when it did not.

The quick victories by the Mongols soon led to a new development in their society. They changed from being a purely nomadic group of fierce cavalrymen raiding settled areas of northern China and elsewhere as they had done for centuries. The emergence of the Mongol empire – the Khanate of the Golden Horde – had transformed the Mongols from attackers to rulers of large dominions with the responsibilities that went with governing vast tracts of land.

The Khanate of the Golden Horde dominated Central Asia and southern Russia from the 1240s for over a hundred years. To govern it, the Mongol rulers encouraged tribes from around

A statue in Elista of the Old White Man, the protector of the universe in Kalmyk folklore.#

# denotes author's photograph.

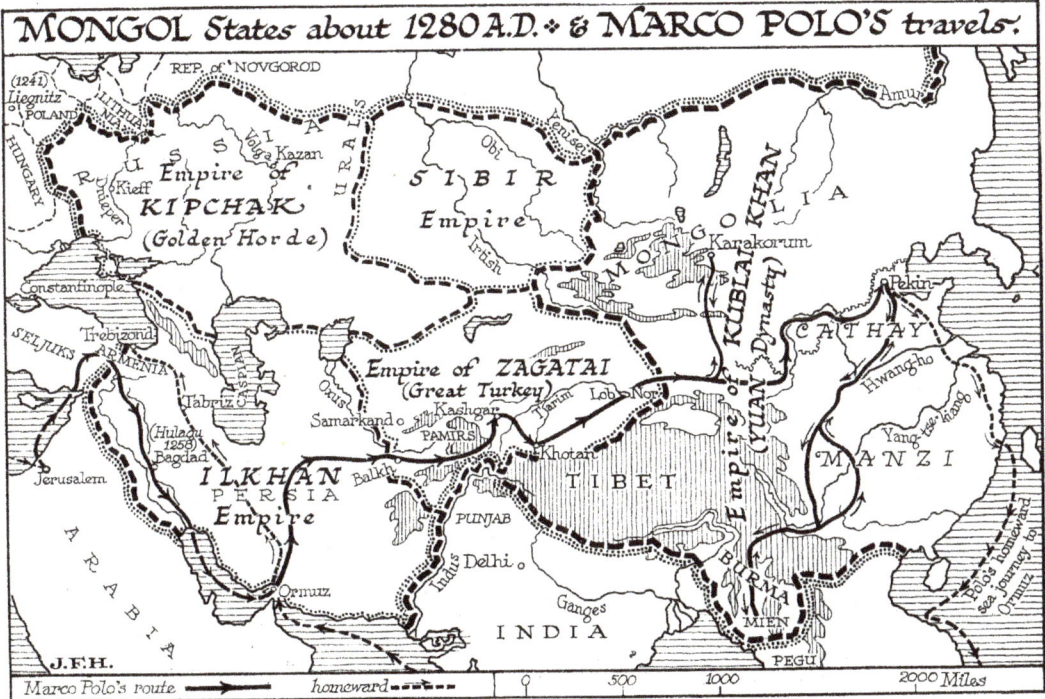

MONGOL States about 1280 A.D. ❖ & MARCO POLO'S travels.

Marco Polo's route →   homeward - - - -   0   500   1000   2000 Miles

J.F.H.

5

Kalmouck

Ivan III 'The Great'.

Mongolia to move to the western part of their newly-established empire. One of these peoples were the Oirats, a nomadic group from southern Siberia, who migrated westwards in search of more fertile land and pasture for their animals. These were the ancestors of the Kalmyks.

The Oirats had come from Dzungaria (Jungaria, now Xinjiang, in China), and they had converted to Buddhism some centuries earlier. Prior to becoming Buddhist, they had a system of beliefs which gave a prominent place to the shamans. These were wise men who treated people for spiritual and medical problems, with a number of customs and traditions, many of which continue through to the present day. By the time they settled in the Steppes, the Oirats clearly identified themselves with the Mahayana Buddhist school. This came about because when the Mongols invaded Tibet in 1239, their leader, Godan Khan, the second son of Genghis Khan, was so impressed with Buddhism that he and his son, Kublai Khan, converted to it. The teachings of the Indian scholar Atisha (982–1054) who had left West Bengal to bring his wisdom to West Tibet became hugely influential in Mongol society and this led to the conversion of the Oirats.

During the fourteenth century, the Khanate of the Golden Horde was devastated by the Black Death, a plague which wiped out vast numbers of the people in the empire, and this, in turn, was followed by massive instability and then civil war, with the empire controlled by twenty-five different khans during the period from 1357 until 1379. This period of strife saw the decline in the power of the Mongols. It coincided with the emergence of Russia under Simeon of Moscow and his successor Ivan II who considered abandoning his allegiance to the Golden Horde but then decided against this. However Tsar Ivan III 'The Great' and his son, Tsar Ivan IV 'The Terrible' managed to break the power of the Mongols around Moscow. With the collapse of the Golden Horde, regional Mongol rulers established their own fiefdoms, and one of these was the Astrakhan Khanate.

The Astrakhan Khanate saw the start of the domination of modern-day Kalmykia from the city of Astrakhan. With its power and wealth, it began to overshadow the region, and this continued through to modern times. The city, located on the delta of the River Volga, meant that merchants there could trade with Persia, using the Caspian Sea, and navigating the Volga, had access to the medieval cities of Kazan (founded 1005), Yaroslav (founded before 1010), and Nizhny Novgorod (founded 1221).

This was the period of the *Dzanghar*, the great epic ballad which describes how the Kalmyks fought their rivals, the

Mangus – a symbolic foe which encapsulated the advantages and evils of their traditional enemies.

Contact with Yaroslav and Nizhny Novgorod brought Russian influences into Astrakhan and it was not long before some of the rulers of Moscow became keen on expanding their lands with Russian rule gradually extending southwards over the region. In 1556 Ivan the Terrible destroyed the Astrakhan Khanate, and built a fort at what is now the city of Astrakhan. This became the administrative capital for Russian power in the region for centuries.

The collapse of the Khanate of Golden Horde, and the later Astrakhan Khanate, had caused many Oirats to return eastwards, with those who remained becoming known as the Kalmyks – the name being a Turkic one for 'remnant' or 'to remain' – in older books the people are often called Kalmucks, or Calmucks. The word appears to have been used for the first time in Arabic by the geographer Ibn al-Wardi in the thirteenth century, with a mention of the 'Kolmak Tartars' by Russian writers in 1530. And the German cartographer Sebastian Münster (1488–1552) mentioned the 'Kalmuchi' on a map in *Cosmographia*, his famous atlas which was published in 1544.

Trade between Kalmykia and Western Europe started during the mid-sixteenth century. One of the major products from Kalmykia sought in Europe was the tulip. These became steadily more popular, especially in the Netherlands, and by the 1630s there was a 'Tulip Craze' in the Netherlands. However although Kalmykia was the original source of these tulip bulbs, the first that most people in Western Europe heard about the region was the emergence of the Kalmyks as fierce soldiers.

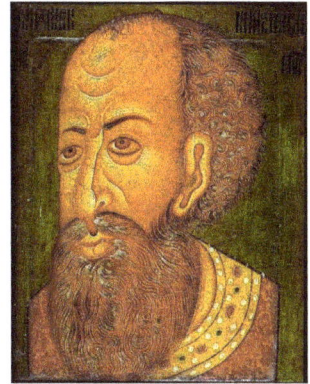

Ivan IV 'The Terrible'.

Nicolaus Germanus's map, *Asian Sarmatia*, 1467. Held in the National Library of Poland.

A Russian postage stamp issued in 2009 to commemorate 400 years of the alliance between the Kalmyks and the Russians.

Scenes from the museum at the Agriculture Faculty of the Kalmyk State University.#

Engagement with Russia

With the departure of so many Oirats, the Kalmyks who remained in what became Kalmykia began to develop a very different culture to that of their predecessors. They changed their belief from Atisha's mysticism to follow the teachings of Jonkhava (Tsong Khapa, 1357–1419), a Buddhist reformer who has been a great influence on Tibetan Buddhism and who emphasised moral and philosophical thinking over traditional mysticism. By the late sixteenth and early seventeenth centuries, Jonghava's form of Buddhism was followed by almost all the Kalmyks, not just the ruling class. It soon was to support the feudal society which was being strengthened in Kalmykia. And this came at the time that Russia started to expand its territory.

The death of Ivan The Terrible in 1584 left a power vacuum. His only surviving son Theodore was unable to rule effectively, and he was succeeded by his brother-in-law, Boris Godunov. In 1604, Tsar Boris Godunov was worried about possible attacks from the south, especially from the Muslim Nogay peoples who lived north of the Caucasus Mountains. The Nogays, allied to the Crimean Tatars, had been supporters of the Astrakhan Khanate which the Russians had destroyed. The Russians were eager to thwart these Muslim tribes from uniting, and as a result the Russians started entering into a tactical alliance with the Kalmyks. The Kalmyks already had a reputation for being particularly warlike, and there was worry at the Russian court that they might, in the long term, emerge as a bigger threat than the Muslim peoples of the region. Indeed the rulers from Bukhara, and from Khiva and Balkh, all had asked the Russians for help against the Kalmyks during this period.

However it was a particularly difficult time in Russia on account of a civil war with various people claiming to be the Tsarevich Dmitriy, the youngest son of Ivan the Terrible. Dimitry had died in suspicious circumstances in 1591, possibly from suicide, although there were claims that Boris Godunov had killed him. When Boris Godunov died, his enemies claimed the boy had actually survived, and endorsed a claimant known in history as the 'False Dmitriy I'. They then staged a rebellion against Boris Godunov's teenage son who was deposed after a reign of only six weeks. False Dmitriy I was crowned as Tsar and he reigned from July 1605 until May 1606. Poland had helped him usurp the throne, and the new Tsar hoped to lead a combined Russian and Polish force in a war against the Ottoman Empire. This necessitated an alliance with the Kalmyks who sent a delegation to Moscow. However before Dmitriy could arrange any major campaign, his opponents took Moscow and killed him. Vasili (or Basil) IV Shuisky from a noble family then became the new Tsar. In spite of his support from the Cossacks and German mercenaries, his rule was by no means certain, especially with the emergence of another pretender known as 'False Dmitriy II'. The failure of several harvests, food shortages and political intrigue, led to a continuation of the civil war.

Tsar Vasili IV signed an alliance with Sweden which helped ensure that Moscow was safe from attack from the north. But this caused Sigismund III of the Polish-Lithuanian Commonwealth to invade from the west. So that he could concentrate his forces to fight the Poles, Vasili IV was anxious to draw up alliances with the peoples of the North Caucasus. He signed an agreement with the Kalmyks on 20 August 1609 – that date being the traditional one celebrated in Kalmykia today for the alliance between the Kalmyks and the Russians although full ties between the two came a little later when the Kalmyks had total control of what is now Kalmykia, and became allies of the Russian monarchy on a continuous basis. The Kalmyks wisely decided to keep out of the Russian Civil War of this period, known as the 'Time of Troubles' which ended with the accession of Mikhail as Tsar in 1613, heralding the start of the Romanov dynasty.

During the 1620s, the Kalmyks sought to expand the area under their control by seizing land around the lower River Volga. This saw the Kalmyks attacking the Nogays and sacking many of their villages. Other tribes in the area also suffered from occasional raids. This began to worry the Russians

Some of the enemies and allies of the Kalmyks:
1 & 2. Circassians; 3. Tatar;
4. Nogay; 5. Turkmen Tatar;
6. Bashkir; 7. Kyrgyz.

who sent in more soldiers, especially to Astrakhan, where the governor, A N Trubetskoi, warned the Kalmyks against attacking any Russian property or people. As a result the Kalmyks left Astrakhan alone, concentrating on the lands to the west of the city. However the Russians became increasingly wary of them.

It was in 1644 that the Muslim enemies of the Kalmyks – the Nogays, the Crimean Tartars and the Kabardinians – finally managed to combine to fight the chief *tayishi* of the Kalmyks, Kho-Urluk. The Nogays and their allies had managed to get a supply of muskets, and they ambushed the Kalmyks at the battle of Karbada, killing Kho-Urluk and his two sons and causing the Kalmyks to flee to the region around the Yaik River. But the victory of the Muslim alliance was short-lived. Four years later the Kalmyks, re-armed and re-energised, drove the Nogays back and seized far more land than they had lost. This led the Russians to point out that under the 1609 alliance between them and the Kalmyks, the Russian state had the right to this land. The new Kalmyk leader Daichin rejected that interpretation and continued harrying the Nogays. By the end of the year the Nogays had been forced to flee to the Crimea, leaving Daichin in control of most of what was now Kalmykia.

By this time the Kalmyks had formed a military alliance of their own with the Don Cossacks, who also viewed the Nogays and Crimean Tatars as their enemies. The Don Cossacks were establishing a close relationship with the Russians, and this once again brought the Kalmyks into an alliance with the Russian state which was now expanding into the Ukraine. The expansion of Russia and these alliances worried Poland which hastily allied itself to the Crimean Tatars. In return the Russians decided to formalise their alliance with the Kalmyks. A written treaty was signed in February 1655 by which the Kalmyk *tayishis* agreed to serve the Russian Tsars. The treaty, in the Russian language, was clearly between the Tsar and a subject people, with the Kalmyks undertaking not to go to war with any allies of Russia, and also provide troops to the Russians in time of war.

A further treaty was signed two years later, granting the Kalmyks even more land, but also stipulating that the Kalmyks could not ally with the Ottoman Sultan nor with the Crimean khans. In 1664 the Kalmyk leader, Puntsuk, received a gilded silver mace from the Russian Tsar Alexis, which was symbolic and later used by the Russians to show that Moscow had the right to appoint the Kalmyk *tayishi*. Puntsuk's son, Ayuki, continued to show support for the Russians who tried to insist that all trade with the Kalmyks had to be routed through Astrakhan or Moscow.

Russian irregular cavalry in the eighteenth century:
1 & 2. Don Cossacks; 3. Kalmyk;
4. Cossack from the Urals;
5. Cossack from the Black Sea;
6. Albanian.

Ayuki had been born in Dzungaria but in 1654 his grandfather brought him to Kalmykia and when his father had died in 1672, he managed to unite the various Kalmyk tribes and after two months fighting, his forces vanquished those of the Nogays. This success did seem to encourage him to embark on a slightly independent course. During the 1680s, the Kalmyks did send envoys to the courts of the Ottoman and Persian emperors and in 1690 the Dalai Lama bestowed an award on Ayuki. Then there was an uprising of the Bashkirs, the Russians sent Duke Alexei Ivanovich Golitsyn to try to win back the Kalmyks and by the 1690s these problems had been ironed out, and the Kalmyks were once again the major Russian allies in the region.

During this time, with the Kalmyks starting to be involved

in formal diplomatic treaties, it had been necessary to have a written language. A Kalmyk Buddhist monk called Zaya Pandita Namka-Djamtso, adapted the Mongolian script to make the Kalmyk script which was called *Todo Bichig* ('clear writing'), and was used until 1924.

The Russo-Turkish War started in 1686 with the Russians, in an alliance with the Austrians, the Poles and the Venetians, fighting the Ottoman Turks. The Russians were keen to take control of the Crimea from the Turks. In the latter years of this conflict, the Kalmyks had been very useful for the Russians, and Ayuki clearly saw more could be gained from a stronger alliance with Moscow than a conflict with the Russian Tsars. Ayuki signed an agreement in July 1697 with Prince Golitzyn by which the Russians also committed themselves to various Kalmyk requests. The Russians undertook to prevent the Bashkirs and Cossacks from attacking Kalmykia, promised to assist the Kalmyks in time of invasion, and that they would not restrict the expansion of Kalmyk pasture land. They also undertook not give protection to any Kalmyk dissidents nor to try to convert any Kalmyks to Christianity. The war with Turkey ended hurriedly in 1700 with Tsar Peter the Great preparing for war with Sweden which broke out in the same year.

Sweden had long been a major power in the Baltic, and the Russians were determined to end this. The opportunity came in 1697 when Charles XI of Sweden died and his 14-year-old son succeeded him. The Russians allied themselves with Denmark, Saxony and Prussia seeking to take advantage of what they expected would be a weak Sweden. However the teenage King Charles XII of Sweden decided to take on his opponents separately. He launched a surprise attack on Denmark forcing them out of the war. He then turned on the Russians and destroyed their navy. The Swedes then invaded Saxony and took over Poland. It was not until 1708 that Charles XII was confident enough to begin his invasion of Russia. In 1610 the Polish/Swedish prince, Władysław IV Vasa had used Swedish troops when he took Moscow and was crowned as Tsar. But now, nearly 100 years later, Russia was much stronger.

Charles XII recognised that he would not be able to capture and hold Moscow without first having destroyed the Russian army in the field. In 1708, the Swedish army marched into the Ukraine. Only the personality of Charles XII held the army together in the bitter winter of 1708-09, and in early July 1709 the Swedes eventually faced a larger Russian army at Poltava. The Swedes were outnumbered nearly 2-to-1, but their troops

The battle of Poltava
by Pierre-Denis Martin,
Catherine Palace, Tsarskoye Selo.

were all veterans and when the Swedish commanders also heard rumours that a large force of Kalmyk cavalry was on its way to the battlefield, Charles XII decided that his best hope was a quick attack.

The fighting began before dawn on 8 July 1709 (28 June, O.S.; 9 July in the Swedish calendar), with the Swedes launching a daring surprise assault on the Russian lines. The Russians were able to deploy their soldiers far more quickly than King Charles XII had expected. Because there were more Russian soldiers than Swedes, the Russians outflanked the invaders and defeated them by noon. There were some 3,000 Kalmyk cavalry at the battle and these were used to harass the retreating Swedes who were forced to surrender three days later. The power of the Swedish army was broken, and Sweden never again posed a threat to Russia.

One of the Swedish army officers taken prisoner at the battle of Poltava was Philipp Johan von Strahlenberg (1676–1747). From the German port city of Stralsund, then a part of the Swedish Empire, he was a career soldier, and also a keen linguist. As a prisoner of war, he was sent to the town of Tobolsk in southern Russia, and he lived there from 1711 until 1721. Whilst there, he used his time constructively and decided to find out about the customs of the region which he formed the basis of his book, *An historic-geographical description of the north and eastern parts of Europe and Asia* (1738). This mentions his experiences with the Kalmyks, and is famous because von

Philip Johan von Strahlenberg's book.

13

A Kalmyk camp.

Peter the Great with Ayuki khan, 1722. Painting by O K Keyyv, 1979.

Peter the Great discussing with Kalmyk leaders in 1722.
A painting at Government House, Elista. #

Strahlenberg introduced the concept of the Caspian Sea and the Urals as being the boundary between Europe and Asia.

And while von Strahlenberg was talking with the Kalmyks, there was the emergence of one of the first Kalmyks who became prominent in Russian society. Mikhail Ivanovich Serdyukov (1677–1754) was an hydraulic engineer who was involved in drawing up the plans for the canal at Vyshny-Volochyok.

Another artist's impression of Peter the Great meeting with Ayuki Khan in 1722.

Completed in 1709 it was later to form the basis of the Mariinsk Canal System (now the Volga-Baltic Waterway) which allowed ships to travel between the Caspian Sea and the Baltic Sea.

After the war with Sweden, to make it harder for anybody to launch another attack deep into Russian territory, in 1718 the Russians completed a chain of forts north of the Kalmyk lands centred on the Volga River port city of Tsarityn (now Volgograd). This cut off the Kalmyks from some of their summer pastures, and in the following year there were changes afoot amongst the Kalmyk leadership. Ayuki was getting old and infirm, and his son Chakdorjab was seen to be less pro-Russian. At the same time the new governor of Astrakhan, Artemii Volynskii, was worried about a possible conflict with the Kalmyks. Therefore Volynskii asked for the Russian government to consider murdering or poisoning Chakdorjab. Whether this happened or not is not known. Chakdorjab was found dead in 1722. He was believed at the time to have succumbed to alcoholic intoxication.

From 1722 until 1724, Russia was involved in a short war with Persia. In this conflict the Russians were now in alliance with the Turks, who promised that the Russians could have control of the North Caucasus region, and also any parts of Persia which they managed to conquer during the conflict. Once again Kalmyk cavalry served in the Russian army. Peter Henry Bruce, a military adventurer whose grandfather had left Scotland during the English Civil War of the 1640s, had himself served in the Prussian army before moving to Russia where he accompanied their army against the Turks. Of the Kalmyk soldiers, he wrote,

> As to their persons, they are of low stature and generally bow-legged, occasioned by their being on horseback, or sitting with their legs [crossed] below on horseback. Their faces are broad and flat, with a flat nose and little black eyes, distant from each other like the Chinese. They are of an olive colour, and their faces full of wrinkles, with very little or no beard. They shave their heads leaving only a tuft of hair on the crown.

In 1726 Vasily M. Bakunin (1700–1766) was appointed the secretary of Kalmyk affairs at the department of foreign affairs in Moscow – briefly again the capital of Russia from 1728 until 1732. An ethnologist and writer, he had served in the Volga region for twenty years and had established good relations with many Kalmyk nobles. In 1737

A detail from the painting opposite, showing Peter the Great's admiral, Denis Kalmykov, the commander of the Kronstadt fortress.

Denis Kalmykov, by V. Montyshev.

KALMUCS.

2.3. Modern Kalmucs.

the Kalmyks in Stavropol under Princess Taishina, established a Kalmyk school in the city.

In the meantime Ayuki had died in late 1722. With the death of his older son in February 1722, when he had met Peter the Great at Saratov, he had asked for another son, Tseren-Donduk to become his successor. Tsar Peter had agreed to this, and on the death of Ayuki, the Russians in Astrakhan supported the claim of Tseren-Donduk. However Prince Donduk Ombo, the son of Ayuki's oldest son, also wanted to be the Kalmyk Khan and his forces managed to prevail.

The next western visitor to Kalmykia arrived soon afterwards. John Cook, a Scottish physician, was in indifferent health, and his doctor had suggested a change of climate. As a result, in 1736 Cook had gone to Russia and joined the medical service of the Russian government, remaining with them until 1750. While he was there, von Strahlenberg's book was published, and Cook's own account, *Voyages and Travels through the Russian Empire, Tartary, and part of the Kingdom of Persia*, was published in Edinburgh in 1768. Cook wrote:

The Kalmucks properly inhabit that great desart (sic) lying betwixt the rivers Volga and Don, having Circassia on the south, and the line, already described, running betwixt the Volga and the Don on the north. They till no land, but feed their numerous flocks. They have no fixed place of abode, but emigrate from one place to another continually, living in tents made in the form of bee-hives; the better kinds are covered with felt, and the poorer sort with rushes or reeds. The Kalmucks live in the borders of Circassia in the winter season, but, when the spring advances, they proceed northerly, even to Tsarizin [Volgograd], and return back again as the winter draweth nigh. There are many different hoards (sic), tho' they are all one kind of people, seemingly without mixture; every hoard has a chief but all their chiefs are subject to one prince called Chan [Khan]. Their Chan constantly keeps a resident in Astrachan [Astrakhan], to take care that his subjects have justice done to them; and a captain presides over a cantoir, where many writers and interpreters are kept in pay for that purpose.

The Russians pretend that they are subjects of their empire; the Kalmucks deny that altogether, but alledge (sic) that they are happy in being under their protection. The Russians keep a resident at the Chan's court, with 2 or 300 soldiers, that he may represent everything necessary to the Chan. It was Donduk Ambo who reigned over them when we arrived in Astrachan. This prince kept very good order, and was a severe disciplinarian: there were very great robberies in his days, but when any happened to be brought to him, who had committed heinous crime, he caused [to] break their arms and legs, and let them be exposed to the wild beasts, without meat or drink, till they expired. They profess the religion of the Chinese, and pay worship to idols, but acknowledge that they are only idols to express the great regard they have for some of their saints. They acknowledge only one God, keep holidays, and have no unbecoming way of worship. They praise God by vocal and instrumental music, having at such times books in their hands, the notes of which are wrote from the top to the bottom of the page. Their music consists of stringed instruments and cymbals, to which they beat time, and indeed it is by no means disagreeable. They have a spear about eight feet long, headed as other spears, broad and double gilt; the neck of the head is encompassed by a ring, to which a leather thong is fastened of about a foot long, the end of which a piece of lead or other metal is made fast. When they worship, one placeth the end of this spear on the ground, and by an imperceptible motion of the hand, causeth the metal turn round, during the time of their worship. Upon enquiry, they informed me that this rotation was an emblem of eternity.

They certainly believe in a future state and have some singular rejoicing in the time of new moons, by building a small tower of earth, placing on it vessels filled with oil and other materials, which they set fire to, and to which exhibits light of different colours, round which they dance, gamble and sing. They marry only one wife at once, nor must they know other women during their marriage state. Their ceremony of marriage is reasonable, though not agreeable to the customs of any other country I know. It is thus: a young pair, agreed betwixt themselves, retire and live as man and wife for one year. If the young woman produceth a child in the space of one year, the marriage is completed and lawful; but it not, they either make another year's trial, or part: not is the woman in the least reflected upon; she is greedily picked up for another trial by others, as if she were a young virgin…

Their priests never marry, but then they have a right, by their law, to go into any man's wife for a night. The men are so far from resenting this, that they take it as a very great honour done to them. Their priests have no riches, for they are free to use anything belonging to any of the Kalmucks as their own property. They make pilgrimages to China, for instructions and benedictions from their lama or high priest.

Calmouk.

ARMS and DRESS of a CALMOCK.

Upper: Engraved by William Grainger for John Hamilton Moore, *A new and complete collection of voyages and travels: containing all that have been remarkable from the earliest period to the present time; ...* (1785).
Lower: Re-engraved for Millar's *New, Complete & Universal System of Geography* (1785).

Another British visitor at this time was Jonas Hanway, a merchant with the Russia Company who wrote *An Historical Account of the British Trade over the Caspian Sea* (1753). He reported that the 'Khalmuck Tartars … are in friendship with the Russians so long as they awe them by their power'. Hanway made his fortune in Russia and then returned to England where he is said to have been the first Londoner to carry an umbrella. But in spite of several people writing of their customs, it remained in war that the Kalmyks were to become well-known, and also most valued by the Russians.

The Kalmyk Cavalry

The outbreak of the Seven Years War in 1756 saw the Russians on the side of the Austrians and the French against the Prussians under King Frederick II 'The Great', and the British. At the start of the war there were some 2,000 Kalmyk cavalrymen in the

Kaiserl. Russisches Militaire.

Russian cavalry: 1. Bashkir, 2. Kyrgyz, 3. Kalmyk, 4. --, 5 & 6. Nogays, 7-9. Cossacks.

Russian armed forces, and the Russian commanders deployed them extensively as they felt that the Asiatic appearance of the Kalmyks would terrify the Prussians. In spite of them often being armed only with bows and arrows, the Kalmyks were decisive in a number of engagements.

Prussia had started the fighting essentially in 1740 when Frederick the Great had invaded and annexed Silesia. The Prussians had won that conflict which became known as the War of Austrian Succession and had ended in 1748. However the Austrians were keen to retake Silesia and eight years later forged an alliance with France and Russia. There was little likelihood of Russia itself being invaded and the Russian military strategy was to invade Prussia and try to capture Berlin. This saw a Russian army advance into East Prussia when, at the Battle of Gross-Jägersdorf on 30 August 1757, a smaller Prussian force attacked them. As the soldiers deployed for battle, the Kalmyk cavalry feigned a retreat, and the Prussians then advanced too quickly and consequently were defeated. However soon afterwards a smallpox epidemic broke out in the Russian army and many of the soldiers, including a large number of the Kalmyks, succumbed to disease and the Russians were forced to withdraw to winter quarters.

In January 1758 Count Villiam (or William) Fermor (of British-German ancestry) led another army of 45,000 Russians into East Prussia, and Pastor Täge of the town of Marienwerder, 40 miles south-east of Danzig (now Gdansk) wrote of being woken up one morning to see Cossacks and Kalmyks in the town:

The Battle of Zorndorf (1758), by Alexander Kotzebue.

> … proceeding down the streets with their long beards and grim faces, and armed with bows and arrows and other weapons. The sight was at once alarming and majestic. They rode through the town in silence and good order ... and we were actually less afraid of the Cossacks than some other armies we had seen pass through Marienwerder. They gave us not the slightest cause for complaint, since they were maintained in exemplary discipline.

The Russians were still aiming to capture Berlin, and the Prussians moved to prevent this. After months of manoeuvring, on 25 August 1758, the Russian commander, Count Fermor, faced the Prussian army under Frederick the Great at Zorndorf. Fermor expected an attack from the north, but the Prussians conducted a night march and appeared on the south of the Russian lines. To try to delay the battle until he could reorganise his soldiers, at 6.30 am, Fermor sent the Kalmyks and Cossacks into action, burning down a village which lay close to the Prussian lines. The Prussians, undaunted, then advanced through the village of Zorndorf and the two armies clashed. The Russians lost nearly half their men when night-time stopped the fighting, and the Russians, short of ammunition, pulled back two days later. Both sides claimed victory but the Prussians had prevented another Russian attack on Berlin.

1752

1. FILLE KALMOUK. 2, 3 ET 4. FAMILLE TATARE.

For a third time the Russians tried to attack the Prussian capital. The opposing forces met at the Battle of Kunersdorf on 12 August 1759. This time it was the Russians who sent in their Austrian allies and were then able to launch a surprise attack on the Prussians. Although this was driven back, the Prussian army was shaken and then the Russian commander, Pyotr Saltykov sent in his cavalry which included the Kalmyks. The cavalry broke the Prussian line and Frederick the Great suffered one of his rare defeats. However the Russians and Austrians lost so many soldiers in the battle and as a result they were not able to make the most of their victory.

The situation in the war changed soon afterwards. In 1761, the Russian Empress Elizabeth died and her nephew, Peter III, who became Tsar, was an admirer of Frederick the Great. He withdrew his country from the conflict, and in 1763 the Prussians and the British won the Seven Years' War. By that time, there was much interest in the Kalmyks in the West.

The Frenchman Jean Chappe d'Auteroche (1722–1769) was sent by the French Academy of Sciences to Tobolsk in Siberia to watch the eclipse of the sun. It was during his time in Russia that he visited Kalmykia writing of the isolation of the region, and also of political developments:

> The revolution which has lately taken place among the Kalmuck Zongors is a remarkable proof that there are very important events which happen in this part of the world, entirely without our knowledge. This nation which occupied an extent of country larger than the kingdom of France, was destroyed by the Chinese in 1757, after a ten year war. During all this time, and till the year 1761, this event was known to the Russian Empire only. All the rest of Europe was ignorant of this revolution; and I was informed of it only as I was travelling through Siberia by some of the Kalmucks themselves, who had escaped the fury of the Chinese, and by some Russians living in Siberia.

Jean Chappe goes on to provide an interesting description of the Kalmyks:

> The Kalmucks, or Eluths, are divided into three principal branches: the Kalmucks Zongors, the Kalmucks Koskotes, and the Kalmucks

KALMUCS REMOVING.

Kalmyk Tartar women, by P. du Halde. Prepared by Jacques Nicholas Bellin, for Antoine-François Prevost, *L'Histoire Generale des Voyages,* The Hague, c.1750.

Torgautes: the Kalmucks Zongors are the objects of our present consideration. This nation was situated in the southern parts of Siberia, extending from 90 to 120 degrees of longitude; and from the 35th degree of latitude, to the 48th, or thereabouts; including in this extent of country several neighbouring provinces, and the lesser Bucharia, which the Kalmucks had conquered in 1683.

The Kalmuck Zongors were governed by a Kam [khan] invested with absolute power, distinguished by the name of Contaisch. He was considered as the chief Kam of all the Kalmucks, and though the other branches of the Kalmucks had their particular Kams, yet they were all in some measure subordinate to the chief Kam, and used to supply him with troops in time of war.

All these people encamp under tents; and are divided into hords (sic) or tribes, under one chief called Taiska.

The Kam of the Kalmucks Zongors resided upon the river Ili, which empties itself into a lake named in the Kalmuck language Balkach-nour, or as some authors call it Palkai-nor; it is situated in 97 degrees of longitude and 46 of latitude.

These people became so powerful under the reigns of the Tsagan-Araptan-chon-taidji, and of his son Galden-Tcheren, and the Russians and the Chinese were afraid of them. The armies which these Kams maintained consisted of about a hundred and fifty thousand men, during the several wars they carried on with great success, for the space of forty years, against the Chinese, the Tangoutes, the Russians, and other neighbouring powers.

Kalmykia is the home of the only native wild camels in Europe.#

In 1766 Chappe was sent to California, again to observe the transit of Venus (with the British despatching Captain James Cook to Tahiti for the same astronomical event). Chappe died in Mexico in 1769, his book, *A journey into Siberia*, made by

ÉMIGRATION FORCÉE DE KALMOUKS EN CHINE.

Publié par Pagnerre, éditeur.

order of the King of France, being published posthumously in the following year.

The Exodus

Although the Kalmyks had fought at Poltava and in the Seven Years' War, there were still many lingering tensions between the Russians and the Kalmyks – the former expecting to use the latter as an irregular cavalry like the Cossacks, and the latter keen to gain further concessions in return. The Kalmyk leaders wanted larger subsidies to be paid to them, and they came to resent various Russian attempts to convert them and their peoples to Christianity. By this time they had also lost their lands on the east of the Volga River because of the rise of the Kazakhs, and some Kalmyks decided that it was time to leave their territory in what had become Kalmykia, and return to Mongolia, a place still cherished in their folklore. Concerned about the shrinking of their lands in the Steppes, several leaders started agitating for a return to Dzungaria (Jungaria, now Xinjiang). This was to divide the Kalmyks.

It was soon after the visit of Jean Chappe, Catherine II

A statue of a mournful Kalmyk woman at the crossing of the Volga, commemorating the Exodus of 1771.

'The Great' started her plans to tap the industrial potential of the Volga region. More Russians, and also Germans, moved into Kalmykia. The Empress also demanded, in 1770, that the Kalmyks provide 20,000 cavalry for her forthcoming war with the Ottoman Empire. This caused the faction within the Kalmyk leadership which urged a return to Mongolia, to win the argument. In January 1771, some 31,000 families – probably 150,000 people altogether – started moving eastwards, heading towards Dzungaria in China, leaving some 11,000 families behind. The folklore relates that the tribes reached the River Volga which was frozen, and on January 4, with most of them on one side of the river, a storm blew up and turned the river into a torrent stranding some on the west bank, and these had to return to their pasture in Kalmykia.

Those who headed to Dzungaria, in China, were attacked by Kazakhs *en route*, losing their herds of cattle, and some being killed. This exodus of the Kalmyks was described in a Chinese state paper which was said to have been written by the Emperor Qian-long (Ch'ien-lung) himself, and a French translation, *Monument de la Transmigration des Tourgouths des Bords de la Mer Caspienne dans l'Empire de la Chine*, was published by the Jesuits in Beijing in 1776 in their *Mémoires concernant les Chinois*. This work attracted much attention in the West, and Edward Gibbon even refers to it in his *The Decline and Fall of the Roman Empire* (1776–88). Much of the rest of the story came from the book by Benjamin Berggmann written in

Dzungaria in the nineteenth century.

Hut of a KALMUC of Eminence.

1804–05, and published first in German and then in French. The Kalmyk exodus was soon to become a famous part of English literature with the publication, in 1837, of Thomas de Quincey's *Revolt of the Tartars, or Flight of the Kalmuck Khan* which appeared initially in *Blackwood's Edinburgh Magazine*, and in book form only in 1896.

The Revolt of the Tartars, or Flight of the Kalmuck Khan

There is no great event in modern history, or, perhaps it may be said more broadly, none in all history, from its earliest records, less generally known, or more striking to the imagination, than the flight eastwards of a principal Tartar nation across the boundless steppes of Asia in the latter half of the last century. The 'terminus a quo' of this flight and the 'terminus ad quem' are equally magnificent – the mightiest of Christian thrones being the one, the mightiest of pagan the other; and the grandeur of these two terminal objects is harmoniously supported by the romantic circumstances of the flight. In the abruptness of its commencement and the fierce velocity of its execution we read an expression of the wild, barbaric character of the agents. In the unity of purpose connecting this myriad of wills, and in the blind but unerring aim at a mark so remote, there is something which recalls to the mind those almighty instincts that propel the migrations of the swallow and the leeming or the life-withering marches of the locust. Then, again, in the gloomy vengeance of Russia and her vast artillery, which hung upon the rear and the skirts of the fugitive vassals, we are reminded of Miltonic images – such, for instance, as that of the solitary hand pursuing through desert spaces and through ancient chaos a rebellious host, and overtaking with volleying thunders those who believed themselves already within the security of darkness and of distance ...

Many of the Kalmyks who did make it to China were met by the Chinese who insisted that they quickly assimilated with their men being forced into the Chinese army. The result was that it

From Rev Thomas Bankes, *A new, royal, authentic and complete system of universal geography, ancient and modern: including all the late important discoveries made by the English, and other celebrated navigators .. and containing a ... history and description of the whole world ...* (London 1787–90).

CALMUC TARTARS.

was not long before these lost their sense of national identity. One part of Kalmyk folklore noted that they had replaced a rope yoke for an iron one. Those who remained behind in Russia are the ancestors of the current Kalmyk population – with, in October 1771, the Kalmyk khanate being abolished by decree of the Russian government.

Although the story of the torrent which prevented some of the Kalmyks from returning to China remains an important part of Kalmyk folklore, it was not the only factor which led to the split in the Kalmyk community. One should not underrate the influence of N A Beketow, the governor of Astrakhan. In November 1771 he had heard that many of the remaining

1. FILLE KALMOUK. 2, 3 ET 4. FAMILLE TATARE.

Kalmyks were leaving and ordered them not to cross to the east bank of the Volga. He also offered them the land which had been used by those who had departed. Why he did this is not certain. It seems likely that the Russian government saw that a large Kalmyk population working for the Chinese could turn on them and be used to invade the region. And those who were under Russian rule had provided cavalry in several wars. Whatever the exact reason, those Kalmyks who were left behind were amply rewarded. Their leader, Prince Aleksei Dondukov was given much land and hailed as their new *tayishi*.

After The Exodus
Prince Aleksei Dondukov was a son of the khan Donduk-Ombo. As a boy, he, his mother, and some siblings, had gone to St Petersburg where they had converted to Christianity. In the early 1760s he then returned to inherit some of his father's land. The prince saw great merit in forming an even closer alliance with the Russian government, but this one was on a strictly subservient level with the Russians abolishing the titles of the 'Kalmyk khan' and 'viceroy' in an imperial decree dated 19 October 1771. Most Kalmyks then fought alongside the forces of Catherine the Great against the rebels in the Pugachev Revolt of 1773-75 when a Cossack claimed to be Peter III, Catherine's husband whom she had murdered in 1762. To gain support, Pugachev promised to free serfs, and managed to build up a large, and well-led army which included some Kalmyks. Catherine the Great also raised a large army which she sent against them, with Kalmyk cavalry being decisive in the routing of Pugachev's men. There were a number of Kalmyks who sided with Pugachev, and these were to be emphasized in the histories of Kalmykia written during the Soviet Union.

Although Prince Aleksei Dondukov had become a Christian, there were still many tensions over Kalmyks being converted to Christianity, and this proved to be a major area of friction. These debates over religion appear to only have affected the Kalmyk elite as the majority of Kalmyks remained nomadic and away from missionary influences.

By the time of the death of Catherine the Great in 1796, the Kalmyks in Kalmykia were an integral part of the Russian Empire, with many Kalmyks serving in the Russian cavalry in the same manner as the Cossacks. Russian leaders had also divided the Kalmyks into the 'White Bone' – the aristocracy; and the 'Black Bone' – the peasantry. In 1803 a 'Guardian of the Kalmyk People' was appointed, and the Kalmyk lands were

Uomo Calmuco
nel Imperio di Russia .

Homme Kalmuque
dans l'Empire Russien .

From Teodoro Viera, *Raccolta di 120 stampe, che rappresentano, figure, ed abiti di varie nazioni, secondo gli originali, e le descrizioni dei più celebri recenti viaggiatori, e degli scopritori di poesi nuovi* (Venice, 1783–91).

30

Donna Calmuca. *Femme Kalmuque.*

Inneres Zelt eines Kalmücken Fürsten, und Herrn Pallas Besuch bey demselben.

Peter Simeon Pallas.

restricted to those between the Caspian Sea and 30 kms from the River Volga.

In 1798, with a significant number of Kalmyk population no longer being nomads, the first stationary Kalmyk *khurul* was built for religious worship – up until then, temples had been in *kibitkas* and were set up and dismantled as the tribes moved around the steppes.

Much more is known about the Kalmyks during the nineteenth century because of the work of a number intrepid Europeans who went to Kalmykia and recorded the customs of the peoples. Peter Simon Pallas (1741–1811), from Berlin, was a zoologist and botanist who, in 1767, had been appointed as a professor at the St Petersburg Academy of Sciences, and from 1768 until 1774 travelled extensively in remote parts of Russia, including Kalmykia, recording his experiences in *Reise durch verschiedene Provinzen des Russischen Reichs* ('Journey through various provinces of the Russian Empire'), published in three volumes between 1771 and 1776. In 1793–94 he was again in the region, going to Tsaritsyn (now Volgograd). Pallas wrote:

> In the environs of Tenatævka we again met with Kalmuks, who were fond of passing the winter here in numerous hordes, but who in the present year had been infected by the small-pox, which was epidemic along the Volga, and obliged them to disperse; this is a disease as dreadful and destructive to them as the plague. According to the latest lists which I received, the remains of this remarkable people, who since the introduction of the provincial governments, and the division of lands, are confined to a more limited situation, still consists of

F. J. J. Bertuch.

Fig.1.

Fig.2.

The Kalmyks in *Bilderbuch für Kinder*, 1792.

Kalmyks from F. J. J. Bertuch's book.

William Richardson.

8,229 Kybitkes, or family tents. Notwithstanding the separation of a large horde of Derbetes who, discontented with their lot, after the extinction of the principal lineage of their hereditary princes, have withdrawn themselves from this district and settled between the Don and the Yaik, where they have associated with the Kozaks; the number of these amounts to 4,900 Kybitkes, or hearths, on the steppe of the Volga.

At the same time as Pallas, another visitor called Benjamin Bergmann also travelled through the region, writing an essay on the Kalmyks, published in 1771, and describing the imprisonment of Mikhail Weseloff in Kalmykia soon afterwards. Bergmann's book, *Nomadische Streifereien unter den Kalmüken in den Jahren 1802 und 1803*, the first to mention the Kalmyks in the title, was eventually published in German in Riga in 1804, and in French as *Voyage de Benjamin Bergmann chez les Kalmüks: Traduit de l'Allemand par M. Moris, membre de la Société Asiatique* in 1825. These works helped inspire Friedrich Johann Justin Bertuch (1747–1822) who, from 1792 until 1830, published his twelve-volume *Bilderbuch für Kinder* which contains interesting images of many different peoples from around the world, including Kalmyks.

And there was a Scottish scholar, William Richardson (1743–1814), who also wrote about the Kalmyks. He was a tutor to the family of Lord Cathcart who was appointed British ambassador-extraordinary to Russia, and took Richardson with him. Richardson preserved letters from his four years in Russia, and these were published in *Anecdotes of the Russian Empire*

(London, 1784). In Letter 52, he describes the Kalmyks who 'subsist by depredation, or by the pasturage of cattle. They pretend they are an independent nation; yet, if they are not absolutely governed, their counsels are much influenced by the authority of the Russians.'

And in the opposite direction, Fyodor Ivanovich Kalmyk (1764–1824) was six years old at the time of the Kalmyk Exodus and had been separated from his family, being captured by some Cossacks who had been sent by Catherine the Great to try to prevent the departure of so many Kalmyks in January 1771. The boy was then one of six children who was taken to St. Petersburg and presented to the Empress. Baptised, he was given the name 'Fyodor', and the surname 'Kalmyk'. As something of a curiosity, she then presented the boy to Friederike Amalie von Hessen-Darmstadt, the older sister of Princess Wilhelmina Louisa of Hesse-Darmstadt (who was married to Catherine the Great's son Paul, later Tsar Paul I). In Hesse-Darmstadt, he was initially trained as a doctor until during classes it was discovered that he had a remarkable artistic ability.

The teenager went to an art school at Karlsruhe in the Grand Duchy of Baden and there he studied drawing, and then travelled to Italy and Greece where he was involved in producing many engravings of Classical ruins and sites. In Rome he worked with Friedrich Weinbrenner (1766–1826), also from Karlruhe. One off Fyodor Kalmyk's achievements in Italy was his famous engraving of Ghiberti's baptistery in Florence. Then in 1803 he accompanied Lord Elgin, the British ambassador to Constantinople, in his famous trip to Athens where work was being undertaken at the Acropolis. This saw Elgin acquire the famous 'Elgin Marbles' which were then sent to England and remain in the British Museum. Kalmyk completed some drawings of the excavations, returning to Karlsruhe in 1806 and became a court painter for the Duchy of Baden.

He travelled to Rome, Naples, Pompeii and Salerno in 1810; and returned to Karlsruhe where in 1813 he was visited by some Russians led Pavel P. Svinyin from the General Staff of the Russian Army. Fresh from the battle of Leipzig, they met Fyodor Kalmyk, with Svinyin writing about this in his subsequent books. Kalmyk died on 27 January 1832 at Karlsruhe.

Fyodor Kalmyk was not the only famous Kalmyk artist of the period. Another was the engraver and artist Alexey Yegorovich Yegorov (1776–1851) remained in Russia where he was involved in work on Russian historical themes.

Abvove: Fyodor Ivanovich Kalmyck, *Self-portrait* (1815).
Below: An engraving from 1845.

Portrait of a young woman, by Alexey Yegorovich Yegorov.

RUSSIE

RUSSIA   RUSSLAND

D

2.
The Modern History of Kalmykia

With several published accounts of the Kalmyks available in Europe, Isaac Jacob Schmidt (1779–1847) enters the story. Born on 14 October 1779 in Amsterdam, the Netherlands, Schmidt was brought up by Moravian parents who had lost their wealth during the French occupation of the Netherlands which started in 1794. A keen linguist, in 1798 Schmidt was offered a position working at Sarepta on the River Volga, in southern Russia. His father then took up a job in Java in the Netherlands East Indies. This left Isaac Jacob Schmidt somewhat isolated in Europe. He decided to adopt Russian citizenship, and became a member of the Russian Academy of Sciences, remaining in Russia for the rest of his life.

Schmidt was considered by his contemporaries to be self-centred and selfish, but he was also one of the first westerners to decide to study the life and culture of the Kalmyks. Through his work with the Moravian church, Schmidt had started making contact with the Kalmyks. He travelled around the Steppes making friends with the chieftains. He soon began compiling records on them and also collecting many manuscripts to do with the Kalmyk language. Up until the arrival of Schmidt, the Kalmyks had been reluctant to let outsiders see any of their precious books, and it was a big pity that they gave them to Schmidt so freely. In 1807 he moved to Saratov and then in early 1812 he went to live in Moscow taking the books and manuscripts with him, intent on writing about them.

Isaac Schmidt.

The Napoleonic War

Although some Europeans had encountered the Kalmyk cavalry during the Seven Years War, it was the Napoleonic Wars which led to much more interest in the Kalmyks who once again were to distinguish themselves as cavalrymen fighting in the Russian army. The Russian armies continued to have a higher percentage of horsemen than most other European armies, and regularly deployed the Kalmyks and the more famous Cossacks as irregular cavalry.

For most of the Napoleonic Wars, the Russians had kept out of the conflict although Tsar Alexander I had sent soldiers to the Battle of Austerlitz in December 1805. Nineteen months later at the town of Tilsit, Tsar Alexander I and the French Emperor Napoleon signed an agreement whereby Russia would not trade

A Kalmyk cavalryman being introduced to Napoleon by Tsar Alexander I at Tilsit.

A Kalmuc Horseman

with Britain.

In 1808, Alexander Arakcheev, the minister of war, had started to modernise the Russian army. As a former artillery commander, he had focused on building up the Russian artillery. Barclay de Tolly, his successor, concentrated on the army. And General N. F. Rtischev had the responsibility of enlarging the cavalry. On 7 April 1811, the Russian government ordered Rtischev to form two regiments of cavalry from Kalmyks living in Astrakhan, Saratov and the Caucasus. The first of these was placed under the command of *Taisi* Tundutov; and the second was under Serebdzhab Tyumen.

With the Russians allowing neutral ships into their ports in violation of the Treaty of Tilsit, and also negotiating for an alliance with Sweden, and peace with the Ottoman Empire, it was clear that war was going to result. Napoleon had found that in his 1807 campaign in Poland, the poor roads hampered his forces, so made considerable plans before his troops crossed the Niemen on 4 June 1812 and invaded Russia.

The forces of the French and their allies had not planned a full scale invasion of Russia. Instead they hoped to be able to defeat the Russian armies and get the Tsar to agree to a new treaty, or at any rate enforce the old one. The Russians, however, retreated ahead of the French, drawing them towards Moscow. On 7 September 1812 the Russian armies finally faced the French at Borodino, west of Moscow. There were Kalmyk cavalry at Borodino, but because the fighting took place over such a small front, they were unable to play any major part because their great manoeuvrability was not as much of an advantage as it had been during the Seven Years' War.

Fresh from the battle, the French and their allies then marched on Moscow which they entered on 14 September. Soon after they arrived, fires broke out in the city, and these all came together in the Great Fire of Moscow on 14–18 September 1812. Issac Jacob Schmidt, the missionary who had befriended so many Kalmyks, fled the city only just ahead of the French troops but he left in his house the precious books and manuscripts he had collected from the Kalmyks. They were all destroyed in the fire. It was a tragic loss.

The fires had been started to deprive the French and their allies of housing and food. The invaders were now unable to hold the devastated city and began a retreat as the weather became worse. It was during this period that the

Kalmyk cavalry played such an important role with them harrying the invaders in October, November and December 1812.

Initially Colonel Antoine-Marcelin, Baron de Marbot, a French cavalry commander, did not have a high opinion of the Kalmyks who still used bows and arrows. He wrote that although they fired 'clouds' of arrows, he only heard of one fatality which had resulted, although he admitted that they did cause many wounds. He was later himself injured by one of the arrows, and on the retreat from Moscow, he came to recognise the terror amongst the French troops from these attacks.

With the French on the defensive after the destruction of their army in Russia, the Kalmyks took part in the attack on the French that followed. On 5 February 1813, the First Astrakhan Kalmyk regiment reached the great fortress of Modlin in Poland. Napoleon had diverted considerable resources towards building a massive fort and some 20,000 people had laboured through 1811–12. It was seen as crucial in a line of defences to prevent any Russian counter-attack, and it was not long before 36,000 Russians were laying siege to the Polish forces who were led by Herman Willem Daendels, a Dutch general fresh from Java. The defenders held out until 1 December 1813 when they were finally forced to surrender. Tundutov was presented with a golden sword by Tsar Alexander I – inscribed 'for bravery'.

In the meantime the Second Astrakhan Kalmyk regiment was deployed at the battle of Leipzig when on 16–19 October 1813, the French were decisively defeated. Napoleon's 'puppet state', the Confederation of the Rhine was then dissolved as the French retreated to the west bank of the Rhine. With the onset of winter, the Coalition of Russia, Britain, Austria, Prussia and others, decided to delay any attack until early the next year.

The coalition plan was to send two large armies against the French in early 1814. That fro the north-east was commanded by the Prussian General Count von Blücher. That from the south-east was placed under the command of the Austrian General Charles Philip, Prince of Schwarzenberg. The First Astrakhan Kalmyk regiment was given to Schwarenberg, and the Second Astrakhan Kalmyk regiment to Blücher. The two forces then attacked simultaneously.

On 24 March 1814, Blücher with the Second Astrakhan Kalmyk regiment, attacked the French at Soissons. On the

Tsar Alexander I in Leipzig, with the Kalmyk lancers on the left.

Prince Tyumen leading the Kalmyks towards Paris.

following day, on 25 March 1814, the Kalmyk cavalry played a crucial role in the Coalition victory at the battle of Fère-Champenoise allowing the Russians and Austrians to advance on Paris. Then, in one of the great moments in Kalmyk history, on 30 March 1814, Prince Tyumen led the Kalmyks in the advance guard of the Russian cavalry which entered Paris, forcing Napoleon to abdicate at Fontainebleau nearly two weeks later.

The departure of Napoleon for exile on the Italian island of Elba led to the Russians standing down most of their army. The cost of the war had been massive, and many of the soldiers had not seen their families for years. The Second Kalmyk Regiment arrived back in Kalmykia on 20 November 1814, and this was followed by the First Kalmyk Regiment on 3 January 1815. Of the original 1,104 soldiers in both regiments, some 734 – about two-thirds – returned home. Some 216 were awarded medals for their role in the capture of Paris, and the two commanders, Prince Tyumen and D. Tundutov had both been given golden swords with the inscription 'for bravery'.

The battle of Fère-Champenoise.

Калмыцкій хурумъ близь Астрахани.

The Khosheutovsky khurul which was built to commemorate the Kalmyks who served in the campaign against Napoleon in 1812–14.

The Nineteenth Century

Although he had lost his manuscripts, Isaac Jacob Schmidt continued his work, being involved in translating parts of the Bible into Kalmyk – improving on an early translation by J Maltschm, and also translated parts of the Bible into Mongolian. His translation was good enough for the British and Foreign Bible Society to encourage a translation of the entire Bible into Kalmyk. Schmidt also wrote extensively on Kalmyk and Mongolian linguistics but soon came to concentrate on Christian evangelical work with the Kalmyks.

Following the end of the Napoleonic Wars, there were many changes in Russia. In 1822, an administrative reform saw the status of Kalmykia raised to that of being equal to an *oblast*, effectively under self-government and administered by the Russian Minister of Internal Affairs, but still with the military governor of Astrakhan playing an important role.

Interest in the Kalmyks continued apace, and in 1821 an English language edition of *Narrative of the Chinese Embassy to the Khan of the Tourgouth Tartars in the Years 1712, 13, 14 & 15 by the Chinese Ambassador, and Published by the Emperor's Authority at Pekin* was published in London. This included a detailed description of the Kalmyks in the early years of the eighteenth century. By this time there was also another book entirely devoted to the Kalmyks. By Henry Augustus Zwick and John Golfried Schill, it was entitled *Journey from Sarepta to several Calmuc Hordes or the Astracan Government from May 26 to August 21, 1823, undertaken on behalf of the Russian Bible Society*, and it was published by Holdsworth and Ball, in London, in 1831.

These new books did help inspire the English writer

Thomas de Quincey.

Pushkin and the Kalmyks.

42

The square in the 1970s with the original bust of Pushkin.

ALEXANDER SERGÈYEVITCH PUSHKIN

Thomas de Quincey (1785–1859) in his work on the Kalmyk exodus, although de Quincey drew more heavily from the earlier works of Pallas and Bergmann. And unlike most of the earlier writers, Thomas de Quincey was well-known in English literary circles on account of his *Confessions of an English Opium-Eater* (1821) and other works. His account of the 'Flight of the Kalmuck Khan' (see p. 27) was published in 1837, and received widespread attention. Many people in Europe had clearly heard of the Kalmyks by this period, and in the previous year (1836), Queen Victoria, in one of her letters referred to members of the House of Orange in the Netherlands looking 'Kalmuck'.

The Kalmyks were certainly also being mentioned in much Russian literature. The Russian poet Alexander Pushkin (1799–1837) made references to the Kalmyk Steppes in one of his poems, visiting Kalmykia in 1829 and meeting Prince Tyumen. And as to the Kalmyk people themselves, he dedicates one of his poems to the 'adorable Kalmyk lass' and in *The Captain's Daughter*, first published in 1836, he relates a story about soldiers including Kalmyks in Orenburg during Pugachev's Rebellion.

Pushkin remains a literary figure much loved by Kalmyks today. He is remembers for noting, 'The Kalmyks had gone from the borders of China under the patronage of the white Tsar. Since then they faithfully served Russia', and his plays are still

The 'Single Tree'.

read in schools all over Russia, and also regularly performed in Kalmykia, with Basang Dordgiev translating *Eugene Onegin* from Russian into Kalmyk. As a result of his connection with Kalmykia, there is also a memorial to him near Government House in the centre of Elista.

At around the time that Pushkin was writing of the Kalmyks, a monk from Mongolia came to visit Kalmykia. He brought with him news of religious and political developments, and also, by tradition, a seed for a tree. This was then planted near the market area which was to become Elista. It was tended over many years and it was nurtured on the barren steppes. Because there are no other trees nearby, it became known as the 'Single Tree'. Kalmyks and foreign visitors from near and far still visit the tree and tie ribbons for good luck and for the granting of wishes.

And while Pushkin was incorporating some Kalmyk ideas into mainstream Russian literature, in 1834 the first systematic attempt to write a history of the Kalmyks was published. Written by Father Iakinth (N Ya Bichurin), and called *Historical review of the Oirats or Kalmyks from the fifteenth century to the present time*, it draws from Russian sources and also provides much information from oral sources.

However the mid-nineteenth century was to see a major change in the life of the Kalmyks. At the start of the century, the overwhelming majority of Kalmyks were living in their traditional tent called the *kibitka*, not much different from the Mongol *gher*. However by the middle of the century some of them had started to make wooden and earthen homes for the winter months, and some of the wealthier ones had brick houses. There were also quite a number of Kalmyks who were marrying Russians. One of these was Anna Alexeevna Smirnova whose family had converted to Christianity. She was thirty when she married a fifty-year-old bachelor and former serf from near Astrakhan called Vasili Nikitich Ulyanov. They had five children before Vasili died in 1836. Their third son Ilya Ulyanov was the father of Vladimir Ulyanov, better-known as the Communist leader 'Lenin'.

Tsar Alexander I whose army had played such a vital role in the destruction of Napoleon died in 1825 and he was succeeded by his younger brother Nicholas I. The new Tsar totally rejected the idea of having a constitution or making liberal reforms. He wanted to maintain the authority of the Tsar, and although he did flirt with the idea of abolishing serfdom, he decided not to do so, and instead maintain the *status quo*, building up a large network

of police spies and informers.

As some of the elite and middle class in St Petersburg and Moscow wanted reforms, more Kalmyks started giving up their nomadic existence for a settled lifestyle. Xavier Hommaire de Hell (1812–1848), a French geologist, in his *Travels in the steppes of the Caspian Sea, the Crimea, the Caucasus etc* (1847) notes a visit he made to a Kalmyk prince and princess:

Xavier Hommaire de Hell,
Revue de l'Orient Vol 5 (1849).

> The little island belonging to Prince Tumene stands alone in the middle of the river. From a distance it looks like a nest of verdure resting on the waves, and waiting only [for] a breath of wind to send it floating down the rapid course of the Volga. But, as you advance, the land unfolds before you and the trees form themselves into groups and the prince's palace displays a portion of its white façade and open galleries of its turrets. Every object assumed a more decided and more picturesque form, and stands out in clear relief, from the cupola of the mysterious pagoda which you see towering above the trees, to the humble kibitka glittering in the magic tints of sunset. The landscape, as it presented itself successively to our eyes, with the unruffled mirror of the Volga for its framework, wore a calm, but strange and profoundly melancholy character. It was nothing we had ever seen before; it was a new world which fancy might people as it pleased; one of those mysterious isles one dreams of at fifteen after reading the Arabian Nights; a thing, in short, such as crosses the traveller's path but once in all his wanderings, and which we enjoyed with all the zest of unexpected pleasure.

In connection with his meeting the Kalmuck prince, Hommaire de Hell wrote:

> After the first civilities were over, I was conducted to a very handsome chamber, with windows opening on a large verandah. I found in it a toilette apparatus in silver, very elegant furniture, and many objects both rare and precious. My surprise augmented continually as I beheld this aristocratic sumptuousness. In vain I looked for anything that could remind me of the Kalmucks; nothing around me had a tinge of couleur locale; all seemed rather to bespeak the abode of a rich Asiatic nawab; and with a little effort of imagination I might easily have fancied myself transported into the marvellous world of the fairies as I beheld that magnificent palace encircled with water, is exterior fretted all over with balconies and fantastic ornaments, and its interior all filled with velvets, tapestries and crystals, as though the touch of a wand had made all these wonders start from the bosom of the Volga! And what completed the illusion was the thought that the author of these prodigies was a Kalmuck prince, a chief of those half-savage tribes that wander over the sandy plains of the Caspian Sea, a worshipper of the grand Lama, a believer in the metempsychosis; in short, one of those beings whose existence seems to us almost fabulous, such a host of mysterious legends do their names awaken in the mind.
>
> Prince Tumene is the wealthiest and most influential of all the Kalmuck chiefs. In 1815 (*sic*) he raised a regiment at his own expense,

The Khosheutovsky khurul, c.1850.

A Kalmyk dance in the presence of Prince Tumene, c.1850.

Grand-prêtre kalmouk avec son ghepi ou chef des cérémonies.

Calmuck Tartars.

and led it to Paris, for which meritorious service he was rewarded with numerous decorations. He has now the rank of colonel, and he was the first of this nomade (sic) people who exchanged his kibitka for an European dwelling. Absolute master in his own family, (among the Kalmucks the same respect is paid to the eldest brother as to the father,) he employs his authority only for the good of those around him. He possesses about a million desiatines of land, and several hundred families, from which he derives a considerable revenue. His race, which belongs to the tribe of the Koshots, is one of the most ancient and respected among the Kalmucks. Repeatedly tried by severe afflictions, his mind has taken an exclusively religious bent, and the superstitious practices to which he devotes himself give him a great reputation for sanctity among his countrymen. An isolated pavilion placed at some distance from the palace is his habitual abode, where he passes his life in prayers and religious conference with the most celebrated priests of the country. No one but these latter is allowed admission to his mysterious sanctuary; even his brothers have never entered it. This is assuredly a singular mode of existence, especially if we compare it with that which he might lead amidst the splendour and conveniences with which he has embellished his palace, and which betoken a cast of thought far superior to what we should expect to find in a Kalmuck. This voluntary sacrifice of earthly delights, this asceticism cased by moral sufferings, strikingly reminds us of Christianity and the origin of our religious orders. Like the most fervent Catholics, this votary of Lama seeks in solitude, prayer, austerity, and hope of another life, consolations which all his fortune is powerless to afford him! Is not this history of many a Trappist or Carthusian?

The position of the palace is exquisitely chosen, and shows a sense of the beautiful as developed as that of the most civilized nations. It is built in the Chinese style, and is prettily seated on the gentle slope of a hill about a hundred feet from the Volga. Its numerous galleries afford views over every part of the isle, and the imposing surface of the river. From one of the angles, the eye looks down on a

Procédé mécanique pour la prière en usage chez les Kalmouks.

Kalmouk.

(Asie.)

1843.

mass of foliage, through which glitter the cupola and the golden ball of the pagoda. Beautiful meadows, dotted over with clumps of trees, and fields in high cultivation, unfold their carpets of verture on the left of the palace, and form different landscapes which the eye can take in at once. The whole is enlivened by the presence of Kalmuck horsemen, camels wandering here and there through the rich pastures, and officers conveying the chief's orders from tent to tent. It is a beautiful spectacle, various in its details, and no less harmonious in its assemblage.

A Kalmyk medicine man.
Bilder-Atlas, 1860

On 1 December 1849, classes had started in Astrakhan to help train Russian-Kalmyk interpreters, and there was to be much more oversight over events in Kalmykia in the years that followed. This school later developed into a secondary school mainly for Kalmyk boys and it was to play a crucial role in educating many prominent Kamyks including Mikhail Badmaev (see p. 62), Nyman Badmavich Badmaev (see p. 62), Davaev Erendzhen, and also the teacher and educationalist Tseren Petkievich Petkov (1877–1967).

During the 1850s, there were some major changes about to sweep through the Russian society. A growing awareness of the agricultural degredation of the land resulted in a major tree planting campaign with oak, lime, poplar and willow trees planted in 1852–53. And on the military front, Tsar Nicholas

An early photograph of the Khosheutovsky khurul.

Sibirifche Tartarin.   Kalmüden.

CAMEL OF A TARTAR EMIGRANT.

I had destroyed the Turkish fleet and the Ottoman Empire appealed for help from the British and French who were worried about the Russians establishing a large fleet in the Black Sea. This resulted in the Crimean War.

Unlike the previous major wars which had involved Russia, the Crimean War saw the Russians trying to hold fixed positions rather than invading other lands or retreating to draw in their opponents. Most of the conflict on land essentially saw the British, French and Italians attacking Russian bases in the Crimean peninsula. The Kalmyk cavalry had been deployed in previous wars to act as shock troops, but the better rifles and artillery, as well as the nature of the conflict, saw the Russian command barely use the Kalmyks. Indeed the Russian generals did not make as much use of the Cossacks either, except for attacking the British and French lines of communication.

As well as the different nature of the conflict, there was also another and certainly more important reason for not deploying the Kalmyks against the British and French in the Crimea. This was because the Russians feared an attack from the Ottoman Empire in the Caucasus, or an attempt by the Ottomans to stir up the Muslim peoples there. Thus the Kalmyks and many of the Cossacks were posted to guard that region. Fighting there did not eventuate but did mean that the Kalmyks were largely uninvolved in the Crimean War.

It also coincided with a period when the social structure of the Kalmyks was splintering. Two years after the end of the war, Prince Tyumen died. He and his life had been a great inspiration to many Kalmyks and was missed by many. Although references to Kalmyks started to appear in many books in Russia and also Western Europe, outside influences were beginning to have a detrimental effect on Kalmyk family life at a time when many were starting to settle and establish permanent pasture. It was no longer just missionaries keen to convert Kalmyks to Christianity. Merchants brought in alcohol, and travellers and others brought diseases. By the mid-nineteenth century, many Kalmyks were no longer proud warriors that they had been in the past. Better farming techniques had made some idle, with drink and disease taking its toll. In the period 1873–74, some 4% of the population were killed in an epidemic, and in 1876 there was only one doctor in the whole of Kalmykia.

These effects on an essentially nomadic rural population were initially missed by many visitors and writers. The English architect and author Thomas Witlam Atkinson (1799–1861), in his *Oriental and Western Siberia: a narrative of seven years' exploration* (1858) mentions riding with Yepta, a 'Kalmuck' when he was involved in the ascent of the Bielouka. A line engraving in the book shows Yepta dressed in furs. In the United States, Eliakim Littell (1797–1870) and his son Robert Smith Littell (1831–1896) published a number of stories about Kalmyks in their journal *Littell's Living Age*. And the Russian writer K. M. Baer wrote his Caspian Expedition, although this remained unpublished until 1984.

Alexandre Dumas in Kamykia

Another visitor to Kalmykia during this time was Alexandre Dumas. In the spring of 1858 he went to St Petersburg for the wedding of a friend. At the age of twelve, he certainly remembered the Cossacks riding through France. He was already one of the best-known writers in France with *The Three Musketeers* having been published in 1844, and *The Count of Monte Cristo* in 1845–46.

Alexandre Dumas in 1855, three years before he went to Kalmykia.

After his friend's wedding, Dumas went to Finland, and then to Moscow, and finally decided to head down the Volga to Nijni-Novgorod and to Kazan. From there he went to Astrakhan, and on 25 October, he noted,

> ... we saw our first Kalmuck tents, and towards eleven we counted a horde of 30 Kalmucks who had just watered their camels at the river bank. The sky above them was literally darkened by flocks of migrating birds, geese, ducks and cranes. Later the same day we were very interested in two unusual buildings near the left bank, a Chinese pagoda and a castle in a strange architectural style I did not recognise. Around them stood a ring of Kalmuck tents. From our captain we learned that the pagoda was sacred to the Dalai Lama, and the castle was the residence of the reigning prince of the Kalmucks.

KALMUCK DWELLING.

JULY.

MARRIAGE CUSTOMS,—STEPPES OF THE CASPIAN SEA : SCRAMBLE FOR A CALMUCK BRIDE'S HANDKERCHIEF.

On 29 October, Alexandre Dumas met Prince Turenne (whom he called Prince Toumaine). Dumas wrote:

The left bank of the Volga was crowded with Kalmucks to greet us, the landing stage was gay with flags , and as we have in sight the prince's artillery saluted us, our boat replying with its two little cannon.

It was easy to distinguish the figure of the prince, waiting for us on the landing stage, wearing national costume — a white coat, very tight and fastened from top to bottom with tiny buttons, a kind of flat Polish chapska on his head, loose trousers and boots of Morocco leather. I had taken care to make sure of the correct procedure beforehand, and followed it precisely. Since the feast was being given in my honour, I duly went straight up to the prince, threw my arms around him, and rubbed his nose with mine, a gesture which expresses every good wish... Prince Toumaine was a man of 30 or 32, fairly tall and rather fat, with very small hands and feet...

After returning my greeting, the prince stood aside to let me pass, welcomed M Strouvé with a simple hand-shake, and the rest of the party with a bow. The castle was 200 yards from the river bank and a guard of honour escorted us to the open front door, where we were received by the major-domo. He conducted us through the palace until we reached a closed door on which he gave a ceremonial knock. Instantly it was flung open by some invisible means, and we were in the presence of the Princess of the Kalmucks.

She was seated on a kind of throne. Her maids of honour, six to the right and six to the left, were squatting on their heels, all as motionless as statues in a pagoda. The Princess was arrayed in a robe of Persian silk embroidered in gold, open at the front to reveal the bodice of her dress, gleaming with pearls and diamonds. Around her neck she wore a plain linen collar, like a man's, fastened in front with two huge pearls. Her head-dress was square, the upper part consisting of ostrich feathers dyed red, the lower part divided and turned back to reveal her brow. On one side it reached the base of her neck, on the other it raised to the level of her ear, which gave her a delightfully inconsequential air... I thought her as pretty as any Kalmuck princess could be. I approached her to make my bow, but she smiled and gave me her hand to kiss – a signal favour as I learned later.'

Alexandre Dumas then described in detail his visit to the pagoda.

On returning to the castle we found the courtyard crowded with Kalmucks, three hundred or more, assembled to enjoy the feast that the prince was providing in my honour, for which his servants had slaughtered a horse, two cows and twenty sheep. The choicest portions of horsemeat, minced with onion, pepper and salt, are eaten raw as an appetiser, a national dish that the prince asked us to taste... For his visitors, Prince Toumaine had provided the choicest delicacies at his command, meat from a young camel and a six-months-old colt, lambs, chicken, game in overwhelming abundance. When at last we reached the dessert stage, the prince asked me to come to the window, glass in hand, to receive a toast from the Kalmucks still feasting outside. As I appeared they all rose to their feet, each with his wooden drinking vessel in one hand and a half-gnawed bone in the other, gave me a cheer and drank my health...

'"Now," said the prince, "you shall see how a Kalmuck moves house." Our camels, laden with a tent and everything needed by a nomad family, were led forward by the father, mother and two sons. At a word of command the great creatures kneeled while their loads were removed, then wandered off to graze while their owners erected the kebitka... Like all pastoral people, Kalmucks live with the utmost frugality. Milk is their staple diet and bread is almost unknown. They drink quantities of tea, and eau-de-vie made from mares' milk is their luxury. Without a compass or any other contrivance they find their way straight across these immense solitudes with complete accuracy. Their sight is incredibly keen, and even after sunset they can distinguish a rider on a horizon, can say whether his mount is a horse or a camel, and, more amazing, whether he is armed with a lance or a rifle.'

The Freeing of the Serfs

Following the Crimean War, in 1861 there was the Emancipation Manifesto which was the first of the liberal reforms introduced by Tsar Alexander II who had succeeded his father Nicholas I in 1855. The Manifesto freed all the serfs, with 23 million people being given their liberty, and full rights of citizenship – although some serfs in Kalmykia retained their servile status.

The move was welcomed throughout Russia where it was

From Hamilton Smith, *The Natural History of the Human Species* (Edinburgh & London, 1852).

seen as modernising the country – indeed in some areas there were serfs who refused to believe they were free. For the former owners of the serfs, they were paid compensation. Twenty years later, a correspondent for the British newspaper, *The Times* on 28 December 1881 reported the trip of his trip through Kalmykia:

> The Kalmucks we had here fallen in with looked like a poverty-stricken lot, but among their nomadic brethren living on their flocks there must be wealthier classes, for, as we came down the Volga, we took up at Saratov two 'Kalmuck princesses', the husband of one of whom, we were told, owned 10,000 tents or families of slaves, for each of which at the emancipation he received as compensation a ransom of seven roubles, or, altogether, 70,000 roubles, with which, by paying wages to the freed men, he still manages to draw a princely revenue from his flocks. The two damsels came on board in princely attire, wearing high-crowned, gold embroidered caps, black silk dresses with scarlet silk sleeves, also richly embroidered with gold, high-heeled bottines, and a profusion of jewellery about their necks and hands. They had their governess, a German, with them, and a goodly retinue of both sexes, and strutted about the deck looking very much as if they wondered what business any of us common mortals could have on a boat which they honoured with their presence.

Certainly the end of serfdom did not remove the entrenched class system, but it did allow serfs to marry without having to get their landlord's consent, and to leave for the cities, which many did, swelling the urban working class.

For Alexander II, he gained the title 'The Liberator' but there were still many opposed to his rule. A growing number of revolutionaries sought to destroy the Russian Imperial family. One was involved in bombing the Winter Palace in 1880, and in the following year, other members of the radical Narodnaya Volya ('People's Will') movement assassinated Alexander

Волъ отъ Калмуцката червена говежда порода.

II. The group was later to gain the support of a student called Aleksandr Ulyanov, the grandson of Anna Alexeevna Smirnova, a Kalmyk who had converted to Christianity. He was arrested in 1887 for planning the assassination of Tsar Alexander III, and was subsequently executed. This event was to radicalise Aleksandr's brother Vladimir, who was, in 1917, to stage the Russian Revolution.

The founding of Elista

Four years after the emancipation of the serfs, in 1865, the Russian government decided to establish the town (and later city) of Elista. Its location was chosen because it was at the confluence of two major roads, and it had been the location of a local market. With a river, and some low-lying land between bluffs, it was possibe to build houses which could be sheltered from the bitter winter winds.

Elista was to become the administrative, and later political and economic capital of Kalmykia. From its foundation there was a significant Russian population, many intermarrying with Kalmyks, but a large number maintaining their own separate society. It was going to be some years before suitable schools and medical facilities were built.

By this time with the advent of photography, some intrepid European photographers had started to venture into Kalmykia to record what they found, although for the most part what survives from the nineteenth century were still wood-engravings. More images of Kalmyks started to appear in magazines and books in Western Europe, and the economy of Kalmykia had started

Уралъ - Oural. Tomn.

to change. The people moved from being largely self-sufficient nomads, to farmers involved in the breeding of cattle. There were probably some 100,000 cattle at the time, but figures collected by the Russian government show that the numbers of horses and camels dropped considerably during the nineteenth century with massive hardship for the poor. But these statistics may also hide what was really happening in the region. It is likely that with the increased integration of the economy of Kalmykia into that of Russia, more people were turning to growing wheat, rye, oats and barley.

And as well as books on Kalmyk history and culture, there was increased interest from linguists. As early as 1843 a primer of Kalmyk grammar and etymology was printed, and four years later, P. Smirnov had produced a Russian-Kalmyk dictionary. V. Diligensky produced another Russian-Kalmyk dictionary in 1853, and a Kalmyk-Russian dictionary was produced by A Vorontsov in 1888, followed by a Russian language textbook for Kalmyks by I. Yastrebov four years later. One of the most important works on the Kalmyks was also published during this period. I. I. Mechnikov's *Notes on the Population of the Kalmyk Steppe of the Astrakhan governate* (1873) helps detail much of the history of the Kalmyks during the eighteenth and nineteenth centuries. Twenty years later, it was followed up by I. A. Zhitetsky, *Papers about the way of life of the Astrakhan Kalmyks, with ethnographical notes* (Moscow 1893).

With woeful educational and medical services, at around this time, a former Kalmyk soldier established a school, and in 1907 he was also to found a hospital. He was the Kalmyk prince, Dorji Ubushaev who had been born on 2 January 1858 near Astrakhan. His mother had died when he was young and he was brought up by Major Alexei Ahverdova who sent him to a cavalry school. There he felt that his Buddhist beliefs would prevent him from being a soldier, and he was baptised into the

L-R: A Finn from Kazan, a Tatar, a Kalmyk, and three Slav Russians from Nizhni Novgorod, 1888.

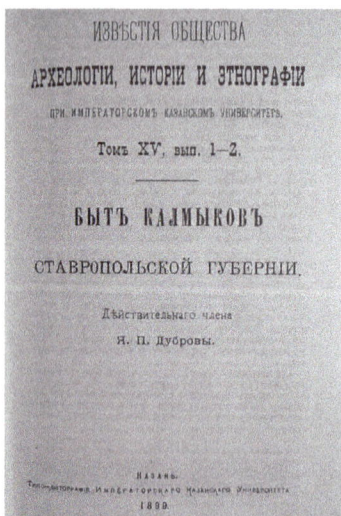

Jacob Dubrova's book on the Kalmyks

Russian Orthodox Church as Mikhail Mikhailovich Gahaevyn, with his godfather being Grand Duke Michael, the son of Tsar Nicholas I and at that time the governor of the Caucasus.

Enrolling with the 17th Dragoons, he had taken part in a number of the battles in the Russo-Turkish War of 1877–78 in a Russian cavalry unit, being awarded the Military Order of St. George 4th class. He then resigned from the army and moved back to Kalmykia and helped develop the local livestock industry and also became involved in forestry. His horses were successful in races around Russia, and he was able to plough back much money into charitable works. Unfortunately he was never to complete all his plans. In 1907, aged 49, he died at Rostov-on-Don. One account has him committing suicide after a major loss during a card game, another has him killed after he shot a local merchant during a commercial dispute, and there is also a version that he was shot by an unknown assailant.

Gahaevyn had started the work, but he was not the only one invoved in projects to improve the lives of Kalmyks. Jacob P. Dubrova had come to Kalmykia after having studied at the Kazan Theological Seminary. A member of the Orthodox Missionary Society which had been established to promote Christianity amongst the non-Christian peoples of the Russian Empire, in 1883 he had gone to Mongolia where he worked with some of the Kalmyks who had left during the Exodus of 1771. Then from 1889 to 1894 he worked as a missionary around Stavropol, teaching Kalmyk children and also becoming fluent in the Kalmyk language. A member of the Society of Archaeology, History and Ethnography at the University of

Kazan, Dubrova presented a number of papers to the society and some of his work was published in the Proceedings of the Society of Archeology, History and Ethnography of Kazan. Dubrova then went to work with the Buddhist Russians in the

АСТРАХАНЬ   Калмыцкій храмъ внутри

A Kalmyk temple from an Astrakhan postcard, 1905.

Altai mountains.

As well as Dubrova, there was an ethnic Kalmyk missionary, Mikhail Badmaev, who also studied at the Kazan Theological Seminary. He had been to the Kalmyk school in Astrakhan, and then the Veterinary Institute in Kazan and then returned briefly to Kalmykia to work before converting to the Russian Orthodox faith, being baptised as Mikhail Vasilyevich, and studying theology in Kazan. He was heavily involved in translating religious works into Kalmyk, finding time to study medicine at the University of Kazan and then to tech there. His *Primer for Kalmyk schools* was published in 1894.

Nyman Badmavich Badmaev was also active in promoting education amongst the Kalmyks. He had been to the same school in Astrakhan as Mikhail Badmaev, and in 1899 he wrote a book of Kalmyk folklore. In 1910 he wrote a Kalmyk-Russian dictionary.

It was a very difficult period not only in Kalmykia but also in much of southern Russia. In 1891 there was a major crop failure in many of the major agricultural provinces in Russia. Initially the government claimed to be unaware of the problems but the writer Leo Tolstoy wrote about it and helped publicise the problem. In an attempt to try to alleviate the hardship for so many people, the government began a series of public works programmes to provide employment for some of the poor. Most of these involved building roads.

The reform law of 15 March 1892 transformed many things with the biggest change being the abolition of serfdom in Kalmykia. It also sought to improve the welfare system in the region – although this remained woefully inadequate. In 1911 there were only three doctors in the whole of Kalmykia. One of these doctors was Simon Zalkind Raphailovich (1869–1941). Originally from Kovno province (modern-day Lithuania), his father was a pharmacist and after completing his high school education, he went to study medicine at Kazan and in 1894 he had moved to Elista and was the only doctor in the town, establishing the first hospital in Elista. Much of his effort was in trying to reduce the prevalence of tuberculosis which was rife.

The British aristocrat, Henry Alexander Munro-Butler-Johnstone (1837–1902) wrote of the situation at the time. The grandson of 13th Baron Dunboyne, he had become fascinated by what became known as 'The Eastern Question', essentially the political problems that were expected to emanate from the impending fall of the Ottoman Empire. A British member of parliament, Munro-Butler-Johnstone decided to visit Russia where he wrote about his time there in *A Trip Up the Volga to the Fair of Nijni-Novgorod* (1875). He wrote:

> On the other side of the Volga, and all along its banks from Tzaritsin [Volgograd] to its mouth, and away westward on the steppes between this river and the Don, the Kalmucks of the Mongol wanders. His mode of life is very similar to that of the Kirghis: the two do not even differ immensely in personal appearance; they are both grimy, but the Kalmuck is the more grimy and glabrous of the two. He is proud of his yellow skin: he has a saying, 'Yellow is gold, yellow is the sun, and yellow is the skin of the Kalmuck.' … books, writing materials, and other signs of culture, of which the Kirghis is wholly innocent, are to be found in the Kalmuck tent. They have schools, too, for the children: for boys long since, for the girls they have latterly established some. The Kalmuck children are precocious and sharp in the extreme; but it has been remarked that if they fail to catch the sense of anything at one, it can never be dinned into their heads. They must learn, as it were, by the 'first intention,' or not at all.
>
> The Kalmuck dress consists of a long shirt, with a loose coat over it fastened with a belt; his boots, when he does not borrow the comfortable high Russian boot, is a shorter red morocco boot with very high heels (but not turned up at the toes), which, whilst it gives him the appearance of being much taller than he is, altogether spoils his walk. The head-dress is pretty and picturesque; it consists of a round Astrakhan woollen hat, like that ordinarily worn by Tartars, with a square piece of yellow cloth stitched at the top, and surmounted with an overhanging red tassel. The women dress very much the same as the men. The children do not dress at all. In the bitterest cold they toddle about stark naked. The further you go into the interior of the Steppes, the wilder and less civilised is the Kalmuck. These are said to be heathen, to eat raw horseflesh, the steaks occasionally cooked as

Djimba Mikulinov was the controversial lama of the Don Kalmyks from 1894 until 1896, he was accused of forging the will of his predecessor Lama Arkad Chubanov, and was removed as the lama of the Don Kalmyks with his replacement not appointed until 1903.

63

a luxury by being placed under their saddles; but the Kalmucks on the borders of, and in contact with, civilization, at any rate, do cook their food. What, however, they never do is to kill their meat. No matter what disease it dies of, the beast must die naturally, and then he is fit to eat. Sometimes, in order to exercise the duties of hospitality, the Kalmuck will kill his meat, and having done so he will eat of it himself, but to satisfy his own requirements never…

In describing the Kalmuck dress, I forgot to mention the well-known fashion of shaving the head, except at the crown, from which their coarse black hair is braided into a queue, which falls down behind.

In 1891 Hans S Kaarsberg, a Danish physician and explorer, went to rural Kalmykia and he noticed the gradual disintegration of the nomadic life over the previous thirty years. Raising cattle was always a hard life, and many were unsuited to the new low-intensity agriculture. Kaarsberg painted a sad picture of the people there, with disease and drunkenness, but still proud of their traditions and the nobility of their forefathers. However, in his book *Gjennem Stepperne og blandt Kalmykkerne* (1892), he noted:

> If the Kalmucks had not in past times helped the Russians, the latter would hardly be what they now are in the Caucasus. The Kalmucks are Russian subjects, judged according to Russian law and are compelled to do military service in the Tsar's army… The horse was once the Kalmuck's wealth, but that time is now past… In past days a well-to-do Kalmuck owned a hundred horses, a rich one a thousands. One

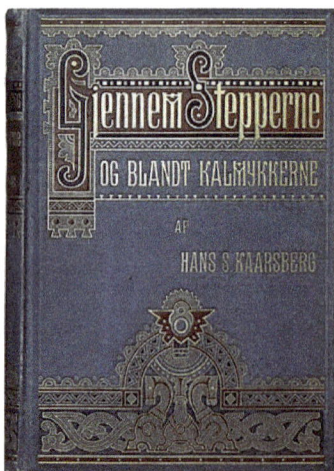

Kalmuck owned three thousand horses sixteen years ago; now he has none at all...

A subsequent foreign visitor to Kalmykia was Samuel Turner (1869–1929), who wrote *Siberia: a record of travel, climbing and exploration* (London, 1905) and *My Climbing adventures in four continents* (London, 1911). In the latter he wrote:

> One of the Kalmucks, whom we met at the last Kalmuck hut, was sitting round our fire when I returned. When my interpreter made me a cup of tea, the Kalmuck handed me a piece of sugar; but after the second cup of tea I found it was a piece of white marble, much to the merriment of the Kalmuck and my party.

He later noted,

> If a man's happiness depends upon the fewness of his wants, the Akkem Kalmuck must be the happiest man alive, especially if what he has is the result of his wanting. I was delighted to be able to distribute some slabs of chocolate amongst the children, who had collected in the hut to welcome the mysterious white strangers. Two of the Kalmucks had come 10 miles to see us. They had never heard of Moscow, St Petersburg or any towns in Europe: Biysk was the furthest any of their friends had been known to travel.

Ovshe Muchkinovich Norzunov, from a Kalmyk noble family, went to Tibet in 1901 and his photographs of Lhasa were the first of the city to be published.

The Kalmyk beef cattle originated in Mongolia and were brought to southern Russia by the Kalmyks in the early seventeenth century.

The major problem facing the Kalmyks was undoubtedly illiteracy. In the All-Russia Census for 1897 only 2.6% were found to be literate, and with a population of 138,582 in the Kalmyk steppe, only thirteen had completed tertiary education, with 68 having finished secondary school education, with an additional eight having completed their secondary education from a military school. But the situation was changing, gradually. Tatiana Jurkova had worked with Simon Zalkind and they opened a school in Elista at the start of 1906, with a girls' school opening on 1 October of the same year. Prior to this boys from wealthier families had to go to Astrakhan, and these two new schools in Elista were to improve the education of Kalmyks. In 1916/17, there were fifteen Kalmyks in tertiary institutions, and by the time of the 1917 Russian Revolution, there were fifty who had completed tertiary courses.

Kalmyks and Russian Politics
The reactionary Tsar Alexander III died in 1894 and his son, Tsar Nicholas II ascended the throne. Ten years later, Russia was dragged into a war with Japan. When it ended disastrously, there were many demonstrations urging for a fundamental change in the nature of Russian government.

Tensions in the cities led to the 1905 'Russian Revolution'

The opening of the Duma, 1905.

which saw Tsar Nicholas II having to make major political concessions, one of which included the calling of a parliament, the Duma. This was to have members elected from every part of the country. The regulations for the election specifically mentioned 'nomadic non-Russians', albeit specifying those who could speak Russian and owned some property.

The first election held in Kalmykia took place in two stages in spring of 1906. In the first stage, in April, people voted for members of an electoral college, with one elector from each settlement. The voters had to be men, aged more than 25, and there was a relatively high property qualification. Then in the following month, a secret ballot was held of the electors, and David Tsandzhinovich Tundutov was elected to represent Kalmykia in the Duma which met in St. Petersburg. He was a Kalmyk nobleman who had attended a number of foreign universities. In the Duma, Tundutov became a member of the Constitutional Democratic Party, better known as the Kadets. This party looked to Britain as their inspiration, hoping to establish a constitutional monarchy in Russia.

Prince David Tundutov (1860–1907).

Tundutov was appointed a member of the Duma's agricultural commission but the Tsar dissolved the Duma, and in January 1907, in spite of the bitter weather, a fresh election was held for delegates for a new electoral college to elect a member of a new Duma. The process in Kalmykia was held up because David Tundutov died in March 1907, and it was not until May 1907 that the eleven electors finally met. They chose S-D B Tyumen over the only other candidate, L B Arluyev, and Tyumen went to St. Petersburg where he also joined the Constitutional Democratic Party.

Tundutov had spoken at the Duma in favour of more rights for the Kalmyks, and Tyumen took up this political position. He also urged for measures to help the cattle industry which was now one of the dominant industries in Kalmykia, along with the growing of melons and also tobacco. However the role that the Kalmyks played in St Petersburg was suddenly diminished. The Second Duma was dissolved and the government declared that the Third Duma 'must be Russian in its spirit'. As a result this new Duma excluded all 'migrating non-Russians' and the franchise was restricted to only the wealthiest 15% of the country.

Although the Kalmyks were no longer represented in the Duma, political consciousness had seen the establishment of the Kalmyk People's Banner, a grouping which brought together teachers in Kalmykia, and which, as a group, brought them in

The Kalmuck Encampment at the Imperial International Exhibition, London, 1909.

New Captive Balloon
New Motor-Race Tracks
New Messina Earthquake
New Kalmuck Camp

Prince Danzan Tundutov
(1888–1923).

contact with the National and Territorial Union of Teachers in Russia.

World War I

In 1909, David Tundutobv's son, Danzan Tundutov, represented Kalmykia at the celebrations in St Petersburg for the 300th anniversary of Kalmykia's association with the Russian Empire. Three years later, for the 100th anniversary of the defeat of Napoleon's French forces, there was a flurry of publications of military histories throughout Russia. The Kalmyks had played such an important role that G. N. Prozreitelev wrote *The Military Past of the Kalmyks: the Stavropol Regiment and the Astrakhan Regiments in the Patriotic War of 1812* (Stavropol, 1912). This book names every Kalmyk soldier in the two regiments, and since its republication in facsimile in 1990, it has been used by Kalmyks, many of whom can trace their ancestry back to a soldier who fought in that war.

Three months after the commemoration of the Russian capture of Paris being celebrated, Europe was heading for another major conflict. This came about on 28 July 1914 when Austria-Hungary declared war on Serbia, and the Russians began their mobilisation. With Russia allied to France and Britain, German war plans had focused on the need for Germany to go to war straight after the Russians started mobilising. This would allow them to invade France first, before turning to attack Russia. This was known in advance to all the powers, and thus Tsar Nicholas II was facing a real dilemma when he had to decide on whether or not to start mobilising his army which was already in a state of some preparedness.

The Kalmyk Prince Tundutov was attached to the General

Staff of the Russian Army from July 1914 and according to the memoirs of the German Emperor, Wilhelm II, Tsar Nicholas II had ordered the mobilisation. The Tsar then had second thoughts about this and soon afterwards he telephoned the Chief of the General Staff, General Januskevitch, to countermand his earlier order. Januskevitch wanted war and believed that he would be able to convince the Tsar that war was necessary, telling his emperor that orders had already been given, when, in fact, they had not. As Tundutov later told Kaiser Wilhelm II, 'This was a lie, for I myself saw the mobilization order lying beside Januskevitch on his writing table, which shows that it had not as yet been given out at all'.

The outbreak of World War I in 1914 saw Kalmyks once again enlisting in the Russian army as they had done so many times before. In yet another war, the Kalmyk cavalry was sent into action, often serving as reconnaissance ahead of the infantry as had happened in the Seven Years War, and the Napoleonic War. In a patriotic gesture, the Russian government renamed their capital Petrograd, believing that the name of St Petersburg sounded too German. But in the areas around Kalmykia where the Volga Germans lived, there was little animosity as many of the German families had lived in Russia for generations.

Simon Zalkind, who had established the first hospital in Elista, was called up for military service but soon managed to return to Kalmykia and became involved in a campaign against a plague epidemic which had broken out around Astrakhan. In 1915, he was appointed chairman of the regional department to combat tuberculosis in the Astrakhan province.

Prince Danzan Tundutov

A postcard from an Austro-Hungarian prisoner of war, Eugen Potocsky, from Kalmykia to a relative in Budapest: 'I am informing you that on the 16th, I am going to Ursum in the Vijatka (?) region. It is most likely that I will write certain things about it. I am healthy, Kisses to you, Jeno. Astrakhan 1917, July 12.'

World War I went disastrously for the Russian armies which initially took the initiative and invaded East Prussia. Their advance was not that different from their moves in the Seven Years War. However this time they were decisively defeated in a number of battles, and the military situation quickly transformed with the Germans able to invade Russia itself, capturing the whole of Russian Poland. In the autumn of 1914, Prince Danzan Tundutov toured regional Kalmykia to try to persuade more men to join the Russian army. Accompanying him was the young ethnographer Nomto Ochirov. In 1915, Tundutov was appointed adjutant to Grand Duke Nicholas, the commander of the Caucasian Front.

Tsar Nicholas II took over command of his army, and by the winter of 1916–17, there were strikes and protests breaking out daily in Petrograd. Many Russian intellectuals felt that it was necessary for a change of government.

The Russian Revolution

With the military situation facing the Russians deteriorating, revolutionaries openly started organising in the Russian army and in society at large. This led to street protests during January and February 1917 which put great pressure on the government. Tsar Nicholas II was persuaded that he had to abdicate and he finally did so, ushering in the Russian Revolution of February 1917. This in turn led to a new provisional Russian government which then declared its intention to maintain its commitments to Britain and France, and to continue Russia's involvement in the war. They also promised to hold elections for a constituent assembly. In these elections, for the first time, there were to be no restrictions based on ownership of property, gender or ethnicity. Soldiers, providing they were not deserters, and monks were allowed to vote. With an increase in political ferment, and a new Russian government guaranteeing press freedoms, the newspaper *Izvestiya Kalmykii* started publication, and remains the major paper in Elista today.

Some Kalmyk units came back from the front. They felt that their oath of loyalty had been to the Tsar and he had now been overthrown, they did not need to continue fighting. Prince Tundutov had returned to Astrakhan from the Caucasus front on 16 March 1917 to allow him to attend the celebrations for the 25th anniversary of the end of serfdom in Kalmykia. On 25–26 March in Astrakhan, a Kalmyk Congress was convened by Tundutov and others. It was dominated by the aristocracy, and it authorised the establishment of a 'national army' of

ARMÉE RUSSE – Cosaques de l'Oural
Kalmouk

A Kalmyk horse, 1900.
These proved to be sturdy cavalry
mounts in World War I.

Kalmyks and an alliance with the Don Cossacks. Tundutov did not have everything his own way. During one meeting, he was denounced as a supporter of Tsar Nicholas II and arrested. However he was soon released and on 16 May 1917 he went to Petrograd with Nomto Ochirov to urge for the establishment of an autonomus province of Kalmykia rather than have it made a part of Astrakhan which would see inevitable Russian ethnic dominance. With the possibility of Kalmykia being given significant autonomy, Davaev Erendzhen (1883–1942), a former student at the Military Medical Academy in St. Petersburg, started to draw up some proposals.

During the spring and summer of 1917, the Russian armies again took to the field against the Germans, and were, once again, defeated. In July there was serious unrest in Petrograd and elsewhere, and it was not until September 1917 that preparations for the nationwide elections were finally started. For Kalmykia there was only one candidate. Sandzhi Bayanovich Bayanov was a lawyer who was living in Astrakhan. He had the support of Prince Temir Batikovich Tyumen and the Kalmyk elite. However before the elections could be held, the second Russian Revolution of October/November 1917 led to a major transformation in Kalmyk society. And it was caused by two men of Kalmyk ancestry.

The first of these was a war hero from the Russo-Japanese War. Lavr Georgiyevich Kornilov had been born on 18 August 1870 in Turkestan (modern-day Kazakhstan) during the reign of Tsar Alexander II. There are some queries about his exact ancestry and whether or not his father (or his adopted father) was a Don

General Lavr Kornilov.

71

Ilya Ulyanov (1831-1886), father of Lenin.

Cossack. His mother was Kalmyk, and when he was fifteen the young Lavr Kornilov had gone to the military school at Omsk and then went to the artillery school in St Petersburg. Because of his background in Central Asia, he was chosen to take part in military expeditions to map some of the Russian borders with Afghanistan and Persia. A military intelligence officer there, he was served with distinction at the Battle of Sandepu and the Battle of Mukden during the Russo-Japanese War and then was posted to China as Russian military attaché. He was involved in mapping the Russian-Mongolian border before being posted to Estonia and then to Vladivostock. Captured in World War I by the Austro-Hungarian forces, he escaped and returned to Russia where he became increasingly critical of Tsar Nicholas II. As the only successful commander during the disastrous Russian offensive of June 1917, this saw the provisional government appoint him Supreme Commander-in-Chief with the head of the provisional government, Alexander Kerensky fearing that the Communists might try to seize power.

Soon afterwards General Kornilov became embroiled in what became known to history as the Kornilov Affair. With Kornilov wanting the removal of any political control over his actions, there was soon tension between the general and Kerensky. On the one hand Kerensky had felt that he needed Kornilov to strengthen his hand against the Communists. On the other, Kerensky felt that Kornilov was trying to seize power and might possibly reverse the revolution, and even restore the monarchy. Thus Kerensky decided to dismiss Kornilov, obviously believing that he could outwit the Communists. Very soon Kerensky found himself dealing with another man of Kalmyk ancestry, Vladimir Ilyich Ulyanov, better known as Lenin.

From about the 1790s until his death in 1836, Vasili Nikitich Ulyanov (or Nikolai Vasilievich), the son of a Russian serf, had lived in Astrakhan where he worked as a tailor. When he was young, he had been given permission to leave his village – serfs unlike slaves were then still tied to a particular village rather than an owner. He then moved to Astrakhan in the mid–1810s, and there he met and married Anna Alexeevna Smirnova, a Kalmyk who had been baptised into the Russian Orthodox Church, as previously mentioned. They had five children, the youngest being a boy, Ilya, born in 1831. His father died leaving a young family with the oldest son, Vasili, aged seventeen, becoming a salesman for the Sapozhnikov Brothers who operated in Astrakhan. He became sufficiently wealthy to help his younger brother Ilya to attend Kazan University and train as a teacher of physics and mathematics. Ilya's younger son was Vladimir Ilyich Ulyanov (Lenin). Commentators noted that Lenin's Kalmyk grandmother had given him an Asian appearance, but he never seemed to have taken much interest in Kalmyk society or in Kalmykia itself except for his manifesto of 1919.

Lenin's older brother had been executed for his part in the attempted assassination of Tsar Alexander III, and Lenin himself had spent some time in exile in Siberia, and then overseas, in Switzerland. He had returned to Russia in 1905, but left two years later, and from exile, he started to campaign to bring down the Tsarist government. The Tsar had abdicated essentially because of the defeat of the Russian armies in war, not from the agitation bu Lenin. With the new Russian government dedicated to continuing the war, the Germans had decided to undermine the Russian war effort by allowing Lenin to return to Petrograd in a sealed train in the hope that he would be able to stage a revolution there and remove Russia from the war. Even if the revolution failed, the Germans hoped that Russia could be engulfed in a civil war.

The Germans were not disappointed. Lenin took power on the night of 25 October (7 November, N.S.) by seizing the main buildings in Petrograd. He then faced the problem that the elections were scheduled for November 25. Worried on the one hand that the new constituent assembly might vote his Bolshevik Party out of power, he was also unwilling to cancel

The statue of Lenin in Elista, 2011.#

A house in Elista in 1918.

Menko Bormanzhinov (1855–1919) was born in the Beliavin aimak (Beliaevskaia stanista) in the Salsk district of the Don Cossacks, and had become a novice monk when he was twelve, and then studied under a range of Lamas. In 1883 he became the Lama of the Don Kalmyks, and was the spiritual leader of the Kalmyks in the land of the Don Cossacks. With the Russian civil war, he fled to a refugee camp in the Kuban but returned to Kalmykia where he died from typhus in April 1919.

the election which might cost him the support of much of Russia which was not under his control.

Soon after the Revolution, some parts of the Caucasus tried to declare their independence from the new Communist government. In Georgia, Menshevik Communists took control; and Armenia and Azerbaijan also became, briefly, independent, issuing their own postage stamps to proclaim themselves to the world. In Kalmykia there was a move to declare independence, and indeed the idea to unite with the Cossacks was raised in mid-November 1917. With the winter about to start, nothing was finalised, and at the height of the winter, the Red Army moved into the Steppes.

The Russian Civil War

Danzan Tundutov and many wealthy Kalmyks declared their opposition to the Communists and raised military units from the ranks of former Tsarist soldiers and their supporters. They then joined the Astrakhan Cossack Army but on 25 January 1918, the combined Kalmyk-Astrakhan Cossacks were defeated by the Red Army. Some of the victorious Communist soldiers were members of the irregular cavalry unit formed by Narma Shapshukova. She remained in the cavalry until 1921 and then joined the government service and then went into politics.

In May 1918 Prince Tundutov was in Georgia at a meeting to establish the Federation of Transcaucasia which soon collapsed. He then left Russia and headed to Germany and met with Richard von Kühlmann, the German foreign minister, and then Kaiser Wilhelm II. In his meeting with the Kaiser he

Narma Shapshukova (1901–1978) during the Russian Civil War.

74

related the role of General Januskevitch in causing the war (see p. 69). He received some German support and money, returning to Russia now in the throes of a bitter civil war.

With the Communists in control of Kalmykia, from 1-3 July 1918, the First Congress of the Soviets of the Kalmyk Working Peoples was held in Astrakhan. A second congress was held on 22-25 September 1918. This led to the introduction of the draft to conscript Kalmyks into the Red Army and started the process of establishing Soviet Kalmykia which was finally put into effect by the third congress held on 19-22 December 1918.

The formation of a Communist regional government in Kalmykia brought to prominence a number of men who were to have a major effect on Kalmyk history and culture. Nomto Ochirov had, as already mentioned, accompanied Prince Tundutov on his recruiting campaign in autumn 1914. By that time Ochirov was one of the of the most well-known Kalmyk intellectuals, being the author of numerous works. On 16 May 1917 he had gone to Petrograd to try to lobby the interim government over the plans for the regional subdivisions in the Caucasus as there was worry that Kalmykia might be split or placed under the control of the Russians in Astrakhan. He returned and was placed in charge of the local food council. Then escaping arrest he went to live at his father's farm.

In the spring of 1919 the White Russian army of General Anton Ivanovich Deniken managed to strike back and it occupied much of the Steppes. In Kalmykia there was a breakdown in law and order. In 1919 the father of Elda Mashtykovich Kekteev (1916–1965) was killed by bandits and he was given to an orphanage. In 1932–36, he trained as a vet and was to become a poet, writing the first novel in verse in Kalmyk.

With war ranging in Kalmykia, on 22 July 1919, Lenin made public his special appeal called *To Kalmyk Brothers*. In it he stated that the Communists would help the Kalmyks, and guarantee free and equal development for Kalmykia. He also rallied the other supporters of the Tsar, ending which his declaration ... 'we must set a substantial part of your territory free from the White Guard gangs. The government of workers and peasants, along with the Red Army, are going to liberate your land. However to do so as quickly as possible and with as little bloodshed as possible, the entire Kalmyk people must rise up as one, against the Tsarist generals and the White Guards, and they must help the Red Army crush Deniken.' He went on to note, 'Your land has been seized by conquerors who are fighting

Shurguchi Nimgirov (d. 1920) succeeded Menko Bormanzhinov in 1919. Born in the same area as Bormanzhinov, he took over during the Russian civil war and fled from the Communists and sought refuge with other Kalmyks on the Greek island of Lemnos where he died in 1920.

Kalmyks presenting a petition to the new Communist government, c.1919

to restore the rights of capitalists and landowners. They are helped by British and French capitalists and landowners who oppress hundreds of millions of your co-religionists in Asia.' The Communists also, a few days after making a similar decree to gain support from the Kazakhs, issued another speaking of the 'toiling Kalmyk people.' This stated that no more Russians would be allowed to take over Kalmyk land. However at that point the Communists clearly did not have much support in Kalmykia itself as the Kalmyk Congress of Soviets being held in Astrakhan.

By March 1920, the fighting in Kalmykia had ended leaving the Communists in control, and this prevented the Japanese from interfering – they had been trying to unite the Mongolian people into establishing some form of pro-Japanese state. However the war did spread into Mongolia. One of the more ardent Kalmyk Communists was Kharti Badievich Kanukov (1883–1933) who was from the Don Cossack region. He had joined the 10th Red Army and was in the propaganda and educational department of the political department early during the Russian Civil War. In September 1919 at Saratov, he organised the newspaper *Ulan Khalmg* ('Red Kalmyk'), and translated many writings by Lenin into Kalmyk. In 1921, he helped get Kalmyks to volunteer to serve in the Red army in Mongolia. On his return, in 1925 he was appointed the Chairman of the Central Election Commission of the Kalmyk Autonomous Region, and in 1929 he was promoted to the chairman of the regional committee of Kalmykia. He died on 7 February 1933 in Elista.

One of the more intrepid members of the Red Army during this period was Matsak Tanhievich Bimbaite who was born in 1900 near Astrakhan and had to look after his family from the age of thirteen on the death of his father. He had joined the Red Army soon after the Revolution and in the 1920s had been sent to Mongolia where he had taken part in the emergence of the Communist state there. In 1926 he was sent to Tibet on a secret mission, describing this in his memoirs which were published in 1983.

Although the fighting in Kalmykia had ended, the economy and the infrastructure of Kalmykia had both been wrecked, and the stocks of cattle and other livestock were severely depleted after having been requisitioned by one side or the other. Many of the Kalmyks who had supported Deniken managed to escape to the Black Sea, and from here some were resettled in Belgrade, the capital of the new Kingdom of the Serbs, Croats and Slovenes (later Yugoslavia), with others moving to Sofia (Bulgaria), Prague (Czechoslovakia) and to the French cities of Paris and Lyon.

The flag adopted by the Kalmyk exiles in 1929.

Davaev Erendzhen moved to Belgrade, Yugoslavia, and was able to write his biography of Genghis Khan which was published in 1927 on the 700th anniversary of the death of the great Mongol leader. In 1929, some land was donated by a sympathetic Serbian businessman and Erendzhen collected money to build a Kalmyk Buddhist temple. In 1932 the Kalmyk World Congress met in Prague and they decided to work on ways to preserve Kalmyk heritage. They also adopted a flag which includes the falcon of Chinghis Khan, and also nine yak's tails. Erendzhen died in 1942 in Belgrade.

With the activities of the Kalmyks in exile, the Communists in Kalmykia became obsessed with infiltrators and spies. Nomto Ochirov had been arrested in March 1920 by the Communist secret police, Cheka, and sent to Astrakhan. He had been released on 23 September 1920 only after another Kalmyk, Arashi Chapchaev, had appealed directly to Lenin. This saw him return to Elista where he was appointed deputy to Anton Amur-Sanan, the representative of the Autonomous Region of the Kalmyk people in the People's Commissariat for Nationalities, although he still had enemies on the local government who were going to get their revenge in the early 1930s.

Anton Mudrenovich Amur-Sanan (1888–1938)

Anton Amur-Sanan was from a poor family in rural Kalmykia but at the age of eight had been adopted by some wealthy Kalmyks and when he finished school, he went to the Faculty of Law in Moscow. He was studying there when the February Revolution broke out, and he had then returned to Kalmykia where he had helped to rally the Kalmyks to the Communist cause. When Deniken was in control of Kalmykia, he had gone to live in Astrakhan, returning to take an active part in the establishment of Communist rule in Kalmykia. This saw the convening of a 'workers' congress' which then called for the establishment of the Kalmyk Autonomous Region which was duly created on 25 November 1920.

Prince Tundutov returned to Russia in November 1922 and was arrested on his arrival. However he was released after only seventeen days in prison. He then tried to get a commission in the Red Army but was rejected. On 14 April 1923 he was rearrested and on 2 August 1923 at a closed trial he was sentenced to death and shot five days later. His wife and son Nicholas were allowed to leave for Germany. On 13 March 1993 he was posthumously exonerated for 'lack of evidence'.

For the Kalmyks in Kalmykia, with regional autonomy, their first problem was to draw up boundaries for the new *oblast* (state). This took more than a decade to finalise, and by that time Lenin had died and Josef Stalin had come to power. During the late 1920s there were vast improvements in health care and the education system. There were also a range of newspapers catering to the newly literate population. By 1921 official records note that there were nineteen libraries and six reading rooms in Kalmykia. From 1921 Nicholas Palmov (1872–1934) from Astrakhan had started collecting material for the establishment of the National Museum of Kalmykia which had been formally opened on 23 March 1921.

A major ideoogical problem facing the Communist regime was how to deal with the private ownership of land. There was also little real support for the Communist ideology in Kalmykia. According to their official history, when the Communist Party started organising in Kalmykia in 1918, it had 'a few members'. In 1921 membership, including candidate members, stood at 609. In 1933 it was 3,143.

Stalin started his collectivization policies largely for ideological rather than economic reasons. Its aim was to destroy the wealthier peasant class. When many farm buildings were dismantled to make way for new collective farms, more and more Kalmyks were angered by the changes which seemed

The Communists meeting in Elista in 1928.

Чагинскій дацанъ. № 16.

One of the temples destroyed under orders from Josef Stalin.

to make little sense to them. Their frustrations were vented in village meetings, and through the monks. For Stalin, he simply ignored the first, and destroyed the temples to remove the influence of the latter. The Krestovdvizhensky Cathedral in Elista was also destroyed.

In 1926 Soviet literature noted that 'banditism was finally liquidated' in Kalmykia, a clear recognition that some of the supporters of the White Russians had remained active for the first six years of Communist rule. Then, five years later the 10th Congress of the Kalmyk Soviets stated that 'stone by stone, the indestructible foundation of the Kalmyk Socialist edifice is

Kalmyk wrestling in 1928.

being laid.' However this involved changing the Kalmyk script. Their vertical script, *Todo Bichig*, was replaced with a Cyrillic script which had been developed by Nomto Ochirov in 1923 and introduced in 1925. This was also a time when Tseren Petkov and others started recording Kalmyk folklore with Petkov completing his Russian-Kalmyk dictionary in 1931.

However there was also a destruction of other elements of Kalmyk culture. At the time of the Russian Revolution in

Elista in 1937.

1917, there were several hundred Buddhist temples throughout Kalmykia. By the mid–1930s, all of them had been destroyed.

At the same time as the Kalmyk culture was being eroded, there had been a vast increase in the fields of health and education, and also the infrastructure was improved dramatically. In 1920 there had been fourteen cars in Kalmykia – in 1935 there were 309, and two years later there were 815 – cars being especially important as there was only one railway in Kalmykia. For these cars, roads were built or improved, and telegraph lines connected all the major settlements.

In 1929 there was training for an air corps in Elista with the use of gliders and also the construction of a parachute tower. In 1930 Elista was raised to the status of a town, and to celebrate this, on 16 May 1930, the foundation stone for the government building was laid, with the first water mains in Elista completed by the end of the year. That year also saw the introduction of primary education for all children, and the founding of the Palmov Museum for Regional Studies. The construction of the Laganski fish cannery in 1934 provided employment for many people.

Elista Airport was enlarged and it handled the postal services which were run by Deruluft (Deutsch-Russische Luftverkehrs Gesellschaft). In 1932 Aeroflot was established as the Soviet national airline, and it soon took over most of the routes. By 1937 there were regular flights from Rostov to Elista and then on to Astrakhan.

On 2 November 1935, Kalmykia formally became an autonomous republic – the Kalmyk ASSR (Autonomous Soviet Socialist Republic), with Elista as the capital. However in many ways the reference to 'autonomous' was 'window dressing' as the Soviet government continued to intrude more and more into the lives of all Kalmyks. Collectivisation increased, even more harshly than before, with any remaining temples being destroyed, and farmers who owned more than 500 sheep deported to Siberia. The number of people living in Kalmykia fell not only in real terms by 13,468, but with an influx of Russians, the between 1929 and 1937, the percentage of Kalmyks in Kalmykia fell from 70% to 54%. There were still only 24,000 Kalmyks living elsewhere in Russia so the falling population was not accounted for by internal migration, and cannot be entirely explained by assimilation either. There were definitely killings, and the list of Communist Party officials in Kalmykia who were purged and killed showed that there was real terror there, not just for opponents of Stalin, but also for many of his supporters. It is

Opposite.
Upper: The statue of Lenin in 1937 with his right hand raised.
Lower: The office of the newspaper *Izvestiya Kalmykii in 1937.*

Elista in 1940 with the main thoroughfare, Astrakhan Street (now Lenin Street), and the Rodina cinema clearly visible.

thought that the famine in Kalmykia in 1932-33 caused most of the deaths.

The purges were savage even on members of the small Kalmyk Communist elite. Nomto Ochirov had already been sacked from the civil service on 1 December 1925. He went to stay with his father who ran a farm. This did not stop him being arrested in mid-1929 by the secret police, the OGPU. He was jailed until 23 March 1930 and was then released with an amnesty. However his freedom did not last long and he was rearrested on 11 November 1930. Tried on 5 June 1931, he was sentenced to five years in prison, being released in July 1934. He was arrested again on 5 June 1941 and held until November of that year.

And Anton Amur-Sanan was arrested on 27 August 1937 when he was staying at his cottage at Vnukovo. A thorough search of the place revealed two books by the Communist leader Nikolai Bukharin who had been purged in the previous year. Amur-Sanan was sent to Stalingrad and finally at a closed hearing held on 16 January 1938 at Stalingrad, a secret session of the Military Collegium of the Supreme Court sentenced Anton Amur-Sanan to death, and he was executed straight afterwards.

The Soviet government was increasingly nervous about the possibility of war. In autumn 1938 with military preparations underway, Elda Mashtykovich Kekteev was drafted into the Red Army, and appointed as the literary editor of the Kalmyk radio.

In spite of the purges, there was an attempt at a Kalmyk

ДЖАНГАР

КАЛМЫЦКИЙ НАРОДНЫЙ ЭПОС

ПЕРЕВОД СЕМЕНА ЛИПКИНА

ХУДОЖНИК В. А. ФАВОРСКИЙ

ГОСУДАРСТВЕННОЕ ИЗДАТЕЛЬСТВО
«ХУДОЖЕСТВЕННАЯ ЛИТЕРАТУРА»
Москва 1940

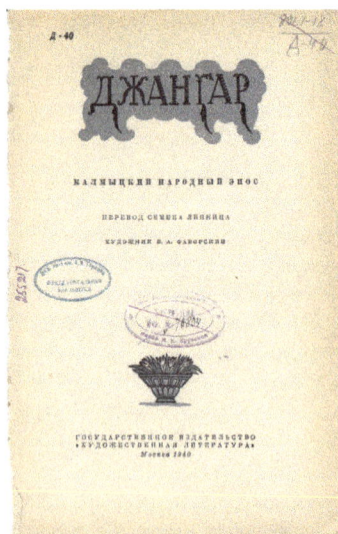

cultural revival from 1938 – in anticipation of the 500th anniversary of *Dzhangar*, with Dawa Shavaliev going to Moscow to start plans for the celebrations, coordinating with Michael Kekedeevich Tyulyumdzhiev. On 28 February – 3 March 1939, the 16th Kalmyk provincial conference was held and later that year. This saw an exhibition in Moscow to celebrate Kalmyk literature in August 1939. Around the same time, Pyurvya Dzhidleevich Dzhidleev (1913–1940), a longtime journalist with *Ulan Khalmg*, was admitted to the Union of Soviet Writers and publishing his collection of poems. Then, in 1940, two 'important' Kalmyk works were published. The first was the great Kalmyk medieval epic, the *Dzhangar,* completed by Shavaliev and Tyulyumdzhiev, helped by Badma Menkenasan (1879-1944), Telta Lidzhiev (1906–1970) who had memorised the entire epic, Mukebyun Basangov (1878–1944), and the Soviet academician Sergei Alexandrovich Kozin; and it was published in the Cyrillic script. Thomas de Quincey had poetically described the *Dzhangar* as being 'seventeen English miles in length'. Written down from the eighteenth century, there had been an extensive study of it by the Russian writer A. A. Bobrovnikov in 1854. By tradition it dates from 1440, and when this new version was published on the 500th anniversary, Stalin had ordered the story to be 'carefully purged' as the original was 'imbued with religious and reactionary content'.

The actual celebrations took place on 6–8 September 1940. At the start the Elista Highway was formally proclaimed open. Symbolically it would connect Elista more easily to the rest of the region. The other work published at the same time was an anthology of poetry of Kalmykia. That ended with an appeal to Josef Stalin to 'lead us on to Communism'. On 1 June 1941, the Kalmyk Research and Development Bureau's institute of languages, literature and history was founded. In its initial incarnation, it was to prove to be short-lived.

3.
World War II, the Deportation
and Rehabilitation

The German invasion of the Soviet Union on 22 June 1941 had a momentous effect on the Kalmyk people, and many other minority nationalities in the Steppes. Twenty months prior to the German invasion, on 23 August 1939, the Germans and the Soviet government had signed a non-aggression pact. Neither side – bitter political foes – could realistically have expected it to last for long, but it bought Stalin some time to rearm and re-equip his forces; and the Germans were able to conquer France.

The Germans attacked at 4 am (Russian time; 3 am German time) on 22 June 1941, and an hour later the German propaganda minister Josef Goebbels announced the German action to the world. With troops from Germany and their allies destroying the Soviet border defences, the population of the Soviet Union was thrown into total confusion. In the late morning, thousands of people gathered in Lenin Square in Elista to hear a radio broadcast about what had happened. At 11.15 am, with Stalin in shock, his foreign minister, V. M. Molotov, the Soviet commissar for Foreign Affairs, made a speech which was broadcast around the Soviet Union by radio, and which was relayed to the people in central Elista on loud speakers. Molotov announced the attack which he said 'is without example in the history of civilised nations'. He noted, 'This war has been forced upon us, not by the German people, not by German workers, peasants and intellectuals, whose sufferings we well understand, but by the clique of bloodthirsty Fascist rulers of Germany who have enslaved Frenchmen, Czechs, Poles, Serbians, Norway, Belgium, Denmark, Holland, Greece and other nations.'

Molotov went on to note that 'The government of the Soviet Union expresses the firm conviction that the whole population of our country, all workers, peasants and intellectuals, men and women, will conscientiously perform their duties and do their work. Our entire people must now stand solid and united as never before.' His 'call to arms' urged the Soviet population to arm to prevent Fascist Germany from invading. Molotov noted that casualties were

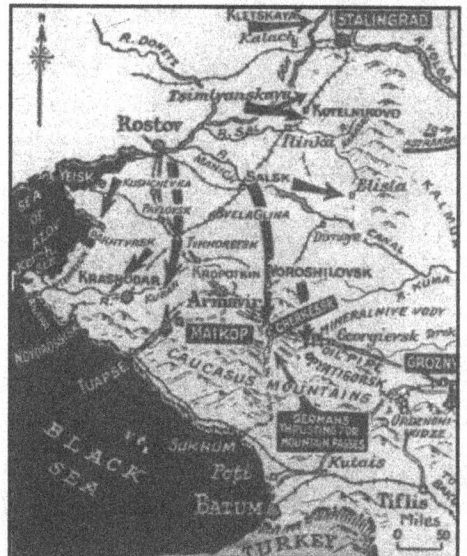

MAIN GERMAN THRUSTS are here shown directed against Stalingrad and south into the Caucasus. On August 17 it was announced that the Russians had abandoned Maikop after, destroying the oil wells. *By courtesy of The Daily Telegraph* PAGE 162

estimated at 200 – only later was the Soviet leadership to discover that they had lost three army divisions (about 45,000 men) on the first day alone. And the Germans claimed to have destroyed 1,489 planes on the first day – the Red Army were to discover that they had actually lost more than 2,000.

Some Kalmyks listening to this speech saw this as their opportunity to gain credit with the Communist government. In the Civil War many Kalmyks had fought on the side of the Whites. This time some community leaders felt that if the population enlisted in large numbers in the Red Army, this might display their loyalty to the Soviet Union. Others undoubtedly hoped that this war might see the demise of the Soviet Union, and for them some genuine autonomy, or even independence. And there were many who recognised the great distances involved and undoubtedly hoped that Kalmykia might remain untouched by the war.

At the start of the fighting, there were already some Kalmyks serving in the Red Army. The most well-known was Colonel General Oka Ivanovich Gorodovikov who had been born in 1879 near Rostov, and became inspector-general of the cavalry in 1938–41. In the fighting in the Crimea in October 1941, Basang Gorodovikov, the nephew of Oka Gorodovikov, also distinguished himself in the harrying of the German soldiers.

In addition to those already serving in the military, 8,664 Kalmyks joined the local militia with the task of harassing any Germans who might arrive in the region. One of those who enlisted was David Nikitich Kugultinov who had been born on 13 March 1922 in the village of Abganer Gahankin. In the 1940, aged only eighteen, he had become a member of the Union of Soviet Writers, a rare honour for a Kalmyk at that time.

For the Germans, their plan had been not to seize cities but to focus on destroying the main Red Army concentrations. Having all but wiped out the Soviet air force, and gaining control of the skies, the German armies were able to advance easily into the Soviet Union. The German Army Group North headed for the Baltic where they were greeted by many of the people there as liberators from a year of oppression by Stalin. Army Group Centre ploughed through the Belorussia, while Army Group South headed for the Crimea. Then the Army Group Centre swung south, cutting off the Red Army in Kiev which was captured on 9 September. By early October, the Germans had pushed the fighting front past Smolensk, with Leningrad (as Petrograd had been renamed in 1924), under siege. By early

Oka Ivanovich Gorodovikov.

Basang Gorodovikov.

December, the German army was close to Moscow when the Russian winter suddenly became even worse than it had been up until then. In January 1942, the Russians were able to launch a number of counter-offensives before there was a lull in the fighting.

Some of the Germans had hoped to gain support from people in the Ukraine and the Caucasus and knew how much hatred there had been to the forced collectivisation in that region. There were also Kalmyks in Germany and other parts of Europe who saw the Germans as possible liberators who might be able to end Communist rule over Kalmykia. Many of these had escaped with the White Russians and now had their first opportunity to return to their homeland. Prince N Tundutov who had fled with the White Russians, was one of those who had planned to return to Elista with the aim of establishing a new government.

The German offensive in spring 1942 had the objective of destroying the Red Army concentrations on the Don River, and then the German Sixth Army would push towards the city of Stalingrad, while the German Army Group A would head for the Caucasus. It was a very ambitious strategy as it stretched the German lines of communication.

As the Germans and their Allies headed south and east, they encountered little Soviet opposition. Hitler assumed this was because the Red Army had been vanquished, not that they were now more easily able to retreat. Stripping the German forces in the south, Hitler, taking effective command, decided to capture Stalingrad. The German military advantage lay in their manoevrability; the Red Army in their ability to harry attackers from fixed positions. Thus the Red Army was to be in a good position to hold off the German attack.

By this time, it was quite clear that the war was going to affect the territory of Kalmykia. Many Kalmyk men were already serving in the Red Army, and Elista was largely undefended when, on 12 August 1942, part of the German Fourth Army arrived in the city. For the first time since its association with the Russian state started in 1409, Kalmykia had fallen to foreign invaders.

The German Occupation

The first German unit to arrive in Elista was the 16th Motorized Infantry. Their task had been to keep open the lines of communication between the Sixth Army and the Fourth Army. Many of the locals were uncertain what to do as the Germans

A War Memorial at Tsagan Aman, 2009. It commemorates by name all the Kalmyk soldiers from that region of Kalmykia who died serving in the Red Army.#

A T-34 Tank as part of a memorial north of Elista. It Tank is monument to soldiers of the 28th Army who liberated Elista.#

90

arrived but there was some resistance and three Red Army soldiers were killed: Lieutenant Eugene Ivanovich Zabolotsky, 2nd Lieutenant Sergei Ivanovich Zus, 2nd Lieutenant Alexander G. Solsylkov, 2nd Lieutenant Sergei Maksimovich Solovyov, Senior Segeant Ivan Alexandrovich Prischena, Private Petr Ivanovich Shpak and Private Novogorenko.

The Germans quickly had to organise billets and commandeered what became known as Red House in central Elista as their headquarters. They were also anxious to secure Elista Airport, north of the city, and the airfield at the town of Utta to the east of Elista.

Just before the arrival of the Germans in Elista, the Red Army and the Communist infrastructure in the city had fled. This had left a dangerous power vacuum because of the remoteness of the city, many of the local people were unable to flee. The arrival of the Germans ended looting and random attacks. Some Kalmyks quickly made money by selling horses to the German army as tens of thousands of the European horses brought by the German army into the Soviet Union had died. The Kalmyk horses were smaller but much more adaptable to the climate which was very hot in the summer, and extremely cold in the winter.

The Germans themselves were always keen on using their own soldiers to fight the Red Army and protect German bases, and did not want to be tied up with local law and order. As a result the Germans often raised a local militia to police areas they had captured.

The commander of the 16th Motorized Infantry was Major Poltermann and he was anxious to raise a local militia unit which would help to maintain law and order locally whilst the Germans adapted the airfields at Elista and Utta for their purposes. Poltermann contacted German headquarters in Poltava where he asked Lieutenant-Colonel Bernd von Freytag-Loringhoven and asked whether there were any Germans who might be able to translate official business messages into Kalmyk. Lieutenant-Colonel von Freytag-Loringhoven was from a Latvian noble family and had grown up in Germany where he had a distinguished career in the army – his cousin was to make the detonator charger for the assassination attempt on Hitler in 1944. After some checking, he nominated Lance Corporal Dr Otto Doll to take over the Kalmyk unit.

Born in Russia, Otto Doll had served in the Austro-Hungarian forces in 1918 and then the White forces during the Russian Civil War before moving to the Sudetenland,

The collective grave in the cemetery in Elista to the six soldiers in the Red Army who died on 12 August, and the one who died on 13 August resisting the Germans.#

The Red House, the German headquarters in Elista.#

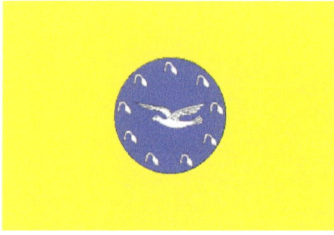

the majority German part of Czechoslovakia – his real name is believed to be Otmar Werve (and he was also sometimes known as Rudolf Verba). In 1938 he had joined the Abwehr, the German Army Intelligence, and with the invasion of the Soviet Union worked at the Abwehr offices at Feodosia, in the Crimea. He spoke Tibetan and as it was similar to the language of the Kalmyks, he was promoted to Sonderfuehrer and sent to Elista where he designed a new local flag.

Dr Doll was not the only German interested in Tibet. Indeed in 1938–39 the German government had financed an expedition to Tibet under SS officer Ernst Schäfer. The aim was, apparently, to search for the possible origins of the Aryan peoples in Tibet – although some historians argue that this was not its central role. However it did create great interest in Germany into Tibet with the team taking some 2,000 colour photographs and 20,000 black/white photographs.

Anticipating that the German advance might lead to the defeat of the Red Army, some Kalmyk exiles from Europe were working with the German forces, mainly operating as German-Russian translators. They headed for Elista and there they urged the local population to join with the Germans against the Red Army. In Elista, and elsewhere in parts of Kalmykia that they had captured, the Germans announced that they were ending the collectivization of land, and that freedom of worship was allowed once again. They encouraged the reestablishment of Buddhism. However at the same time the Germans also sought out the small Jewish population in the city who numbered 93 families – as many as 300 individuals. They were taken by the Germans and some were shot on the outskirts of the city, and others were bundled into train carriages and were taken to the death camps in German-occupied Poland where they were killed. J Otto Pohl in his book *Ethnic cleansing in the USSR 1937–1949* (1999) also notes that the Germans killed some 20,000 people in Kalmykia.

At this juncture, Nicholas Poppe (1897–1992) enters the story. Serving with the German forces in Kalmykia, he had been born in Shandong (Shantung), China, then under heavy German influence – the Germans establishing their colony at Qingdao (Tsingtao) in that year – his father was the secretary to the Imperial Russian consulate at Tianjin (Tientsin), Qiqihar (Tsitsihar), Shenyang (Mukden) and then at Haerbin (Harbin) where he was murdered by a burglar. Poppe was educated at Petrograd

University and then became a professor at the same institution – renamed Leningrad University – where he had been involved in the cataloguing of Mongolian manuscripts. In 1931 with the death of Boris Vladimirtsov, he had taken over the Mongolian Department at the Institute of Oriental Studies. He helped the Red Army demarcate the Mongolian border with the Japanese puppet state of Manchukuo in 1939, and then in 1941 with the German invasion, had moved to Kalmykia where he was living when the Germans arrived. He immediately became a translator for the Germans and said he wanted to write about the minority peoples of the Soviet Union becoming a go-between in the new administration which set up a militia.

Initially there were two squadrons of what was initially known as the Calmuck Legion. Dr Doll was in charge, and he had a German driver and a German radio operator, but apart from them, all the remainder of the men serving in the unit were Kalmyks. These squadrons served more as units allied to the Germans than as 'Free Korps' serving under German control. The recruitment came at a time when it was necessary to maintain law and order against looting and robbery. Many of the Kalmyks in the cavalry units also rode horses, although some used Bactrian camels.

A German propaganda photograph of a Kalmyk, *Signal* magazine.

The task of the Calmuck Legion was to guard the main road leading east connecting Elista with Utta, and also with Chalkuta and Justa. This was the road which terminated at Astrakhan, and the Germans had the aim of capturing that city even though they were already extremely overstretched in terms of the areas they were already holding. Most of the fighting was taking place north of Kalmykia where, at Stalingrad the German Army had captured a large part of the city and had hoped to cross to the east bank of the Volga.

The Calmuck Legion was able to secure the western part of the Elista-Astrakhan road and this allowed German convoys to pass up and down it easily. In fact General Graf von Schwein of the 16th Motorized commented that although the Kalmyks were undisciplined, they did their allotted tasks well. There was a major engagement in December 1942 when some of the Calmuck Cavalry Corps attacked the 59th Destruction Battalion of the Red Army at Ulan Tug, south of Utta, and destroyed half the Soviet unit. Dr Doll by this time had appointed a Mongolian, Baldan Metabon, who had previously served in the Soviet 110th Cavalry

A German liaison officer with Kalmyk volunteers.

A German soldier with a Kalmyk camel.

Division, as his chief-of-staff, and the two of them created great trust among the Kalmyks.

The German occupation was certainly not unopposed by the people in Elista. Yuri Klykov – his name means 'canine teeth' – was only seventeen and had been a student at School No 2 in Elista. He fled to Astrakhan and there he was trained in guerrilla tactics, returning to Elista where, on October 1942 he formed the group called 'Thunder', attacking the Germans but they were surrounded on 5 November 1942, and after holding out for two days, were captured with Klykov taken to Elista where he was tortured, and defiant to the last, was executed on 13 November. There is also an obelisk outside the Red House to commemorate these and others who died fighting the Germans.

At around this time the battle at Ulan Tug became the single largest military engagement of the Calmuck Legion, but it was also to be their last. The war suddenly turned against the Germans. The Red Army had launched a major winter offensive on 19 November 1942 with the aim of pushing the Germans from Stalingrad as winter set in. The Germans recognised that they were stretched too thinly across southern Russia and decided to cut their losses and regroup. In January 1943, the German 16th Motorized Infantry was prepared to be pulled out of Elista, as the Germans evacuated the Caucasus.

When news spread around Elista and Utta that the Germans were going to withdraw, there was mass confusion. Many Kalmyks had trusted the Germans to finally rid them of the Communists and now they clearly felt betrayed. They were given the option of going with the Germans, and into exile like so many Kalmyks had done after the Russian Civil War, or remaining in Kalmykia. In the end, some 10–15,000 Kalmyks chose to leave with the Germans, with 75–80,000 deciding to remain knowing that they would face the fury of the Red Army.

Nicholas Poppe, the Soviet specialist in Mongolia, packed his bags to leave with the Germans.

There were many reasons why so many people decided to remain in Elista. These were not only on account of family ties, and history, but the Kalmyks had seen how those who left in 1920 had been unable to return. However a far greater reason was that although 3,000 Kalmyks served alongside the Germans, far larger numbers of Kalmyks had joined the Red Army and fought for the Soviet Union in engagements in many areas. This meant that many Kalmyks had relatives in the Red Army, and some were members of the Communist Party, with far larger numbers having relatives who were in the party.

As the Germans were preparing to evacuate Elista, the Kalmyk soldiers were formed into ten squadrons, totalling slightly more than 2,000 men. On 18 January 1943, ten Calmuck cavalry squadrons were deployed to east of Salsk serving alongside Cossacks, to guard the German retreat. The retreat itself saw many families having to split up, most knowing that they might never see each other again. As the Calmuck Legion left, the Red Army managed to regroup and entered Elista and Utta. They brought with them a large number of NKVD, the Soviet secret police, who went through the towns searching for anybody who had collaborated with the Germans. Whatever any of the Kalmyks expected, nothing would prepare them for what was to happen in the winter of 1943.

Mikhail Kondikov raising the flag of the Soviet Union once again over Elista.

The Deportation
Although much has been made of the Calmuck Cavalry Corps, only 3,000 Kalmyks had served in the unit whereas 20,000 served in the Red Army. In 1942 Colonel Khomutnikov's Red Army Kalmyk cavalry unit was praised for its actions against the Germans at Rostov. In October 1942 Stalin had sent an open letter to the Kalmyks about 'the determination of the Kalmyk people to mobilize all their resources to help the Red Army rout the invader'. There were references in Soviet newspapers in January 1943 that the Germans had pulled out of Elista, and in *Soviet War News* on 9 February 1943, there was also a mention that the Kalmyk Provincial Committee of the Communist Party had started reopening schools and also collected 7 million roubles for military supplies for the Red Army. Then there was no mention of the Kalmyks in the press for the next fourteen years.

On 27 December 1943, a decree was issued in the name of the Supreme Soviet, the Soviet Union's parliament, and

Mikhail Kalinin who ordered the deportation of the Kalmyks.

The Deportation Memorial in Elista.#

Close to the Deportation Memorial is an old cattle truck similar to those used to deport the Kalmyks.#

The War Memorial in Elista commemorating Kalmyk soldiers and civilians who died in the Great Patriotic War, including those deported to Siberia.#

this announced that the Kalmyk Autonomous Soviet Socialist Republic had been abolished and all Kalmyks were to be deported. Signed by Mikhail I. Kalinin, it was officially Decree No 115/144 of the Presidium of the Supreme Soviet of the USSR, and was entitled, 'On the liquidation of the Kalmyk ASSR and the formation of the Astrakhan oblast within the composition of the USSR.' It was one of a number of orders which were issued by Josef Stalin during World War II. The first, issued on 28 August 1941 had affected the Volga Germans. They were a minority in the Volga region, and the reasons for it were obvious. Then in October-November 1943 the Karachay people, some of whom collaborated with the Germans, were also deported, in their case to Kazakhstan and Kyrgyzstan. Now it was the turn of the Kalmyks.

The decree led to Red Army soldiers and police going from door to door in Elista, and in villages around Kalmykia. There were many Russian-Kalmyk families. For children, if their father was Kalmyk and their mother Russian (or indeed from any other ethnic group), they were deemed to be Kalmyk. If their father was not Kalmyk, then they escaped the deportation. Non-Kalmyk women married to Kalmyks had the choice of divorcing their husbands on the spot, or being deported with them. Many of the people were given thirty minutes to pack their

A book on the deportation of the Kalmyks with a poignant photograph on the front cover.

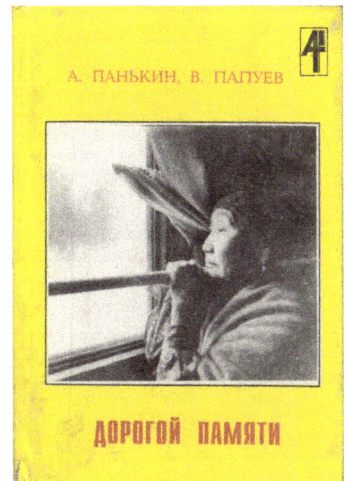

The museum to the Deportation at the Kalmykia Lyceum, 2013.#

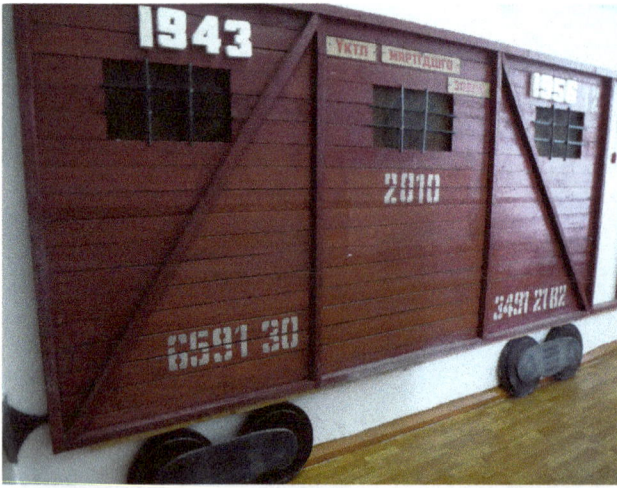

bags to leave. Altogether some 120,000 Kalmyks were deported. Nobody expected the savagery that was to follow. There was no resistance as many of the Kalmyk men were fighting in the Red Army. This meant that a significant number of families being deported had one or more members serving as Red Army soldiers. Some expected that the deportation would be brief, moving them out of the scene of possible fighting. With Kalmykia producing twenty-three 'heroes of the Soviet Union' during the conflict, they could not have anticipated the revenge that Stalin would wreak on account of the very small numbers of Kalmyks who had sided with the Germans.

Like all the other refugees and people deported in World War II, and indeed in earlier conflicts, the Kalmyks had to decide on what to pack. It was winter, so heavy clothes were essential. Decisions had to be made over whether to take practical items or possessions of a more personal nature. One woman took her Singer sewing machine as she told her family that there was always demand for a seamstress. Many lost family photograph albums, books, and papers. Most took papers linking their families to the Soviet regime – details of their own or family member's war service in the Red Army.

Once the Kalmyks in Elista had packed, there was a slow progression of people wending their way to the railway station in the north of the city. There they were forced onto cattle trucks and taken to locations in Siberia. With probably half the population of Elista being forced to leave, of those who remained in a half empty city, undoubtedly it was not long before looting started. Elista was soon renamed Stepnoi.

The Diaspora

Whilst the Kalmyks who had remained in Kalmykia were being deported to Siberia, others had fled westwards with the Germans and were regrouped in the Ukraine. The Kalmyk soldiers were initially given coastal guard duties on the Sea of Azov and then towards the start of March 1943, Field Marshal Paul von Kleist decided that he would merge all the Cossack fighting units at Kherson in the southwest of the Ukraine. He assumed that the Kalmyks were Cossacks and they were sent there, but on their arrival the local commander recognised the mistake and separated them. The Kalmyks were then given 1,000 Dutch rifles and 35,000 rounds. The next time they appear in the surviving German records is on 18 April, when they had a strength of 2,200 men. A more accurate count was made ten days later and it was found that they had 79 Kalmyk officers, 353 NCOs and 2,029 men, as well as 2,030 horses and camels. At that time they were on coastal guard duty at Mariupol.

The decision was then made to move them to Zaporozhye on the lower Dneiper River. On 23 May, another count of them noted that there were 67 Kalmyk officers, 374 NCOs, and 2,917 men. The extra number seems to have been accounted for by more Kalmyks having fled and joined their compatriots, as well as probably a number of the civilians, especially teenage boys, travelling with them officially enlisting. By August the 'Kalmueken Verband Dr Doll' was renamed the Kalmucken Kavallerie Korps (Kalmyk Cavalry Corps). It now had battalions (which were often called 'divisions'). Dr Doll remained the commanding officer, with Major Eduard Bataev (Erdne Dorziev) as his adjutant. Major Baldan Metabon was still the chief-of-staff, and Major Kallmeyer was the liaison officer.

The 1st Battalion was commanded by Major Lukyanov Ciligirov, and consisted of the 1st, 4th, 7th, 8th and 18th Squadrons. The 2nd Battalion was placed under Major Boldyrev Mukubenov, with the 5th, 6th, 12th, 20th and 23rd Squadrons. Major Abushinov Ciligirov commanded the 3rd Battalion which had the 3rd, 14th, 17th, 21st and 25th Squadrons, and Major Konokov Savkaev commanded the 4th Battalion which consisted of the 2nd, 13th, 19th, 22nd and 24th Squadrons. Each squadron had between 120 and 150 men, making the total strength at a little more than 3,000.

The Kalmyk Cavalry Corps served behind the front line and one major engagement in which they were involved was at the Nikopol bridgehead which was where the 4th Panzer Army was stationed, with the Kalmyks guarding the rear of the line. Covering an area some 75 miles long, along the banks of the Dneiper River, it was very swampy and there were numbers of Red Army guerrillas there. The Germans had been in some

Geshe Wangyal.

Kalmyks in New Jersey in 1959.

trouble until the Kalmyks arrived and successfully engaged the guerillas. In one operation they managed to kill 50 Red Army soldiers and capture another 32.

However in spite of the praise for them, some of the Germans did not understand the Kalmyks and were frightened by their appearance. There were Germans who wanted then disarmed, and others who wanted them separated from their wives and families. Dr Doll managed to stop this and in February the Kalmyks were pulled back to Lublin, Poland, where they were still used for anti-guerilla activities, albeit now operating in woodland, hills and marshes. In the following month, Metabon was no longer chief-of-staff.

From May until July, Major Mukeben Chachlysev ran the Kalmucken Kavallerie Korps. In June, the Germans massed their forces for an attack on guerrillas at the Bilgoraj Forest. Even though the Kalmyks fought well, the Germans were still having trouble understanding them. The Kalmyk soldiers had given up their homeland to fight for the Germans, and were aggrieved when food and rations did not arrive on time. They made up for this by taking provisions from local people, leading to complaints to the German command. Dr Doll seems to have managed to get the Kalmyks to serve in the front line again, and they were sent into action against the Red Army. It was to prove disastrous. Although the Kalmyks performed well, as they had always done, Dr Doll and Chachlysev were both killed in action.

Dr Doll had been a father-figure to the Kalmyks, and his death caused immense grief. Initially Oberstleutnant Bergen was put in charge, and then Bataev took control, with Captain Dorzi Arbakov became the new chief-of-staff. On 21 July 1944, the strength of the unit was still very much the same, but they now had 71 German staff, as well as 68 attached to then, with some 3,000 Kalmyks, who had 4,600 horses and camels.

It was not until January 1945 that the Kalmyk Cavalry Corps was sent into action again. By this time it numbered some 5,000 as most of the civilian men and older boys were drafted. However it was badly mauled by the Red Army near Kielce and withdrew through Silesia to Austria in the following month. The unit was then dissolved leaving the Kalmyks stranded in Austria uncertain what to do.

After being in refugee camps in West Germany for a number of years, many of the Kalmyks applied to resettle in the United States. To get around the US immigration policy, the Kalmyks were designated as European (which they were), and described by a friendly US official as 'Caucasian' on the basis that they came from near the Caucasus. Most were resettled in New Jersey.

Nicholas Poppe managed to get an invitation to Cambridge University but was refused a visa to Britain on account of his work for the Germans. He subsequently went to the United States where he wrote reports on aspects of the Soviet Union and led the University of Washington's role in studies concerning Mongolian and Altaic subjects. He published extensively before his death in 1992.

One of the Buddhist priests who worked the Kalmyk community in New Jersey was Ngawang 'Geshe' Wangyal. A Kalmyk Buddhist priest, he had been born on 15 October 1901 in Astrakhan province, the youngest of four children. When he was six he started training as a novice monk and after the Russian Civil War he went to Tibet and studied at Lhasa until 1935 when he decided to return to Kalmykia. However with the Communists having taken over, he decided instead to move to Beijing and after two years in the Chinese capital, he then went to Calcutta where he worked as a translator to Sir Charles Bell, the British explorer. Going with Bell to Tibet, he remained there and fled when the Communists took over Tibet. Moving to the Britain, on 2 February 1955 he flew to the United States on the *Liberte*, and worked as a priest with the Kalmyks who were settling in New Jersey and also elsewhere in the United States. Teaching at Columbia University, and translating some work from Tibetan and Sanskrit, he died on 1 February 1983 in Palm Beach, Florida.

Kalmyks in New Jersey in 1959.

The Heroes of the Soviet Union

Although much has been made of the small number of Kalmyks who collaborated with the Germans, the Kalmyk Republic was to produce the twenty-two Heroes of the Soviet Union, the highest number of any of the republics in the USSR. The most famous remains Oka Ivanovich Gorodovikov who, in July 1941 had been given the temporary command of the 8th Red Army in the North-West but was redeployed to fight at Stalingrad. A deputy in the Supreme Soviet of USSR, he was to be one of the few Kalmyks who was not deported.

His nephew, Basang Gorodovikov had remained in the Crimea where on 1 May 1942 he had been appointed a commander of the partisans, and then as the Germans were pushed back, he took part in the fighting at Sevastopol, and then was moved to the Baltic before taking part in Operation

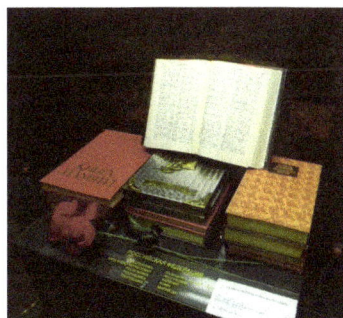

Memorial registers for Red Army soldiers from Kalmykia and nearby regions in the Hall of Broken Glass, Museum of the Great Patriotic War, Moscow. #

Erdni Delikov from an anti-tank company, in the History Museum.#

Erdni Delikov.#

Bagration which saw the Germans pushed back from Belarus, and then from Lithuania. The army was then able to move into East Prussia and General Gorodovikov took the first victory parade of Soviet troops in Germany. However on 2 December 1944 he was seriously wounded and taken to a military hospital in Moscow. After recovering, he resumed his duties. Heavily involved in training the Red Army in the late 1940s and 1950s, he was able to help with the Kalmyks returning to Kalmykia in 1956, moving to Moscow in 1978. He died there five years later and was buried in the Novodevichy Cemetery in Moscow.

In mid-July 1942, a month before the Germans took Elista, Erdni Teldzhievich Delikov became the first Kalmyk to be awarded the title of Hero of the Soviet Union when he used an anti-tank gun to destroy three German armoured cars and then three trucks containing German machine gunners. However he was mortally wounded on 21 July near Rostov.

The others from Kalmykia made Heroes of the Soviet Union all received their awards after the deportation, and their careers illustrate the major difficulties facing the Red Army as it

Nicholas Martinovich Sandzhirov. #

Lidzhi Mandzhiev. #

Akim Gavrilovic Metyashkin. #

slowly drove back the Axis forces.

In August 1943 Nicholas Martinovich Sandzhirov managed to clear nearly seven thousand mines when the Red Army broke out of Novorossiysk and drove back the Germans – he was subsequently made a Hero of the Soviet Union but was killed in fighting in Poland in February 1942.

On the night of 26-27 September 1943, Lidzhi Mandzhiev, a gunner in the anti-tank artillery regiment of the 12th Army was involved in the crossing of the Dnieper River. Attacked by German dive-bombers, one of the Red Army barges was set on fire and Mandzhiev jumped into the water and unhooked it, thereby saving the rest of the convoy. He was later involved in other actions which led to him being made a Hero of the Soviet Union

Akim Gavrilovic Metyashkin had fought at Kursk and was also involved in the fighting around the Dnieper River – the so-called Wotan Line of defence prepared by the Germans – being made a Hero of the Soviet Union in 1943. He died fighting the Germans in the following year. Also for actions when the Red Army recrossed the River Dnieper, N. I. Batashov was made Hero of the Soviet Union for his actions fighting the Germans.

In January 1944, at the height of winter, the Russians launched another offensive pushing the Germans out of

Ivan Germashev.#

A U.S. army map showing the Wotan Line.

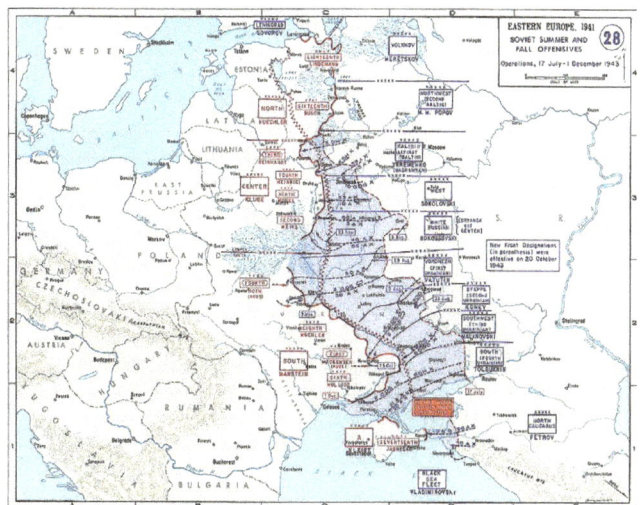

Bator Basanov. #

Stepan Krynin. #

the Ukraine although the Axis forces remained in control of much of Belorussia. In late spring, the Soviet High Command redeployed many of their soldiers to the north and in June 1944, Ivan Germashev took part in the fighting near the town of Rogachev, Belarus. On 24 June he led the attack on the Germans and broke the Axis lines allowing the Red Army reinforcements to win a major victory earning him the award of the title of Hero of the Soviet Union.

On 11 July 1944 in the village of Duhnovo, near Pskov, Sergeant Bator Basanov, a postman before the war, attacked Duchnovo in Latvia, the headquarters of the 19th Latvian Waffen SS division, managing to seize the German regimental colours, being made a Hero of the Soviet Union. After the war he was assigned to Western Ukraine where he fought the nationalists who remained a guerrilla group for several years. He was then posted to Siberia where he was involved in the defences for important military facilities.

To the southwest of the fighting involving Bator Basanov, on 14 July 1944 in Belorussia, Stepan Krynin was able to cut the highway along which the Germans were retreating, and this led to 120 German soldiers being killed with Krynin being made a Hero of the Soviet Union.

The next actions were on the southern front. On 14-21 September 1944 in the village of Poiana in Romania, Fyodor Popov was involved in the bitter street fighting and killed about twenty Hungarian soldiers, crossed the river and held back a major Axis counter-attack destroying several of their tanks. Although injured himself, Popov continued fighting until the Axis forces withdrew. He died on 14 January 1945 near Galsha,

Fyodor Popov. #

Ilya E. Zigunenko. #

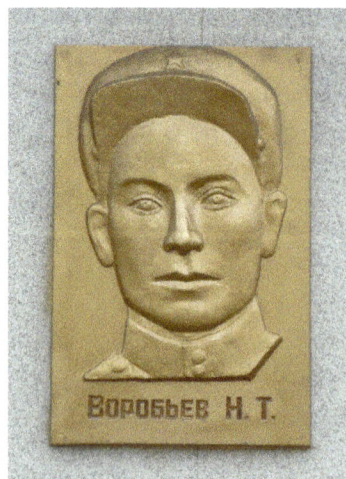

Nicholas T. Vorobiev.#

Czechoslovakia.

From Romania, the Red Army pushed into Hungary, and on 4-5 December 1944 they attacked the town of Ercsi to allow them to cross the Danube. Ilya E. Zigunenko, a Kalmyk from Stavropol, managed to establish a bridgehead on the far bank of the river and clear the way for other units of the Red Army to cross. He was made a Hero of the Soviet Union but died in fighting at Sümeg in western Hungary on 27 March 1945. Nikolay Konstantinovich served alongside Zigunenko in the crossing of the Goluboy Dunay.

On 5 December 1944 Nicholas T. Vorobiev managed to lay a cable across the Danube to allow the Red Army on both sides to communicate with each other. He was killed on 14 February 1945 in the battle for Budapest and was posthumously made a Hero of the Soviet Union.

Further north, Pavel Turchenko who had fought against the Germans in the Ukraine, near Kalmykia itself and then in Belorussia, was proclaimed a Hero of the Soviet Union for his actions in the crossing of the River Vistula in January 1945 and then for his subsequent actions on 14 May 1945. Involved in the capture of Berlin when he was seriously injured, he died in 1987 near Stavropol.

With the Red Army advancing into Germany, on 16 April 1945, Lieutenant Mergasov, a secret service agent, with the infantry, earned himself the award of Hero of the Soviet Union for a range of activities behind German lines. On the same day, Major Anatoly A. Lopatin led his tank corps across the river Spree to form a bridgehead and this allowed many other soldiers to cross the river although Lopatin himself was killed in a German counter-attack on 22 April.

Cyril Matveevich Zhigulskiy was a Kalmyk who had been drafted into the Red Army in 1940. He was assigned to border defence and survived the German shock attack on 22 June 1941. Wounded several times in the fighting that followed, he distinguished himself in the fighting on 19-21 April 1945 at Stettin (now Szczecin, Poland). He managed to cross the Oder River under heavy fire and consolidate the Red Army bridgehead, being made a Hero of the Soviet Union. This resulted in the capture of lands where the Kalmyks had fought during the Seven Years' War nearly two hundred years earlier.

Bemba Mandzhievich Hechiev, a postman before the war, also fought at Stalingrad and in other engagements in the war including the capture of Berlin, becoming a Hero of the Soviet Union for his actions during the attack on the German town of

Pavel Turchenko. #

Anatoly A. Lopatin. #

Cyril Matveevich Zhigulskiy. #

ХЕЧИЕВ Б.М.

Bemba Mandzhievich Hechiev.#

Frivak on 30 April 1945 when he managed to kill sixty German soldiers and destroy a number of gun emplacements.

Exile in Siberia

As the Kalmyks in Germany were moving to the United States, those in Siberia had to live through a long period of terrible deprivation. Soviet secret police chief Lavrenti Beria was to report that the initial deportation of the Kalmyks involved 26,359 families, a total of 93,139 people who were taken away in 46 railway trains. Soviet records note that 2,975 NKVD officers were involved, and they were provided with 1,255 vehicles for the task.

The Kalmyks were taken to southwestern and central Siberia. These were the areas of Altai Krai, Krasnoyarsk Krai, the Novosibirsk oblast, and the Omsk oblast, based around, respectively, the towns of Altai, Krasnoyarsk, Novosibirsk and Omsk. There were 25,000 sent to the areas of Altai krai, 25,000 to Krasnoyarsk krai, 25,000 to the Omsk oblast and 20,000 to the Novosibirsk oblast, based around, respectively, the towns of Altai, Krasnoyarsk, Omsk and Novosibirsk. Horrific stories of what happened to the Kalmyks in Siberia have been recorded. Taken in cattle trucks to Siberia or remote parts of Kazakhstan, they were dumped at isolated railway stations and in railway sidings. It was the middle of the Russian winter, and many quickly succumbed to the cold, illness, starvation, and to broken hearts.

As with all groups of people facing such adversity, the exiled Kalmyks on arrival started to try to hold together their society. Some were lucky to find unoccupied houses or outbuildings, but others had to start from scratch and build their own dwellings. Most managed, amazingly, to find enough food to keep themselves alive. Rumours were spread ahead of them that the Kalmyks were cannibals and as a result many people from Siberia were frightened when the huddled groups of Kalmyks appeared in their villages. Andzhuka Kozaev involved in the 1940 *Dzanghar* epic, died in Siberia a year after being deported, as did the playwright and poet Baatr Badmaevich Basangov.

Kalmyks from the Rostov and Stalingrad oblasts were deported soon after those from Kalmykia, and in early 1944 some 15,000 Kalmyks serving in the Red Army were demobbed and deported. In spring 1944 those Kalmyks living in Ordzhonikidze krai and the Kizlyar district were also deported, and at the same time army commanders and political commissars who were

An exhibit in the old history museum in Elista showing the bleak life in Siberia for the Kalmyk deportees.#

Kalmyks were sent to Tashkent or Novosibirsk where they were demobilised and sent to join their families. There were also soldiers from the front who were sent straight to penal camps. In spite of this, there were also said to be 4,000 Kalmyk soldiers still serving in the Red Army at the end of World War II.

Very soon the Kalmyk deportation was followed by those of other peoples: the Chechens, the Ingush, the Balkars and the Crimean Tatars. All of them were to face similar problems. However as Robert Conquest notes in his book, *The Soviet Deportation of Nationalities* (1960), that the deporting 'of the Kalmyks was the only one involving an entire republic of which no public statement was ever made.' He also noted that Lenin had promised the 'integrity of the Kalmyk territory' but his undertakings 'did not stand the first strains put upon them.'

For the Kalmyks, during their time in Siberia – for thirteen years – half of all Kalmyks died. Family units had started to disintegrate, and children grew up with no firsthand knowledge of any security, with all the Kalmyks having no civil rights. All the Kalmyks were registered by the local officials, and if a relative died, the family members had to bring the body to the police or the person might be suspected of having escaped.

In spite of all the problems facing the Kalmyk society, there was also an attempt to continue to preserve the Kalmyk traditions. Garyaev Odzhakaevich Dordzhin had been heavily involved in cultural activities before the war and since 1937 he had been working with the Kalmyk State Song and Dance Ensemble, being designated an 'honoured artist of the Kalmyk Autonomous Soviet Socialist Republic' in 1940. At the start of the war he moved to work for local theatres and in Siberia he helped to organise a music and theatrical school. He died on 30 September 1946, aged 38.

Certainly the writers who helped to put together the *Dzhangar* in 1940 were not spared. Badma Menkenasan survived for a year in Siberia. And Telta Lidzhiev who was not initially deported because he was fighting at Stalingrad, was also sent to Siberia when he was no longer needed in the fighting.

For some of the deportees, their route to Kazakhstan was rather more circuitous. Sanji Kalyaevich Kalyaev (1905–1985) had trained as a teacher when he was seventeen, and supported the Communist Party for some years before he formally joined in 1928. He produced pro-Communist drama at Saratov but was denounced, expelled from the party in December 1932, but was rehabilitated in the following year. He then worked with the Kalmyk Institute in Astrakhan, and in 1937 was again denounced, sentenced to eight years hard labour for being an 'enemy of the people', being sent to Siberia where he fell ill and was released into internal exile in early 1943. Only then he was deported to Kazakhstan.

Finally, on 5 March 1953, Josef Stalin died. He was succeeded by Nikita Khrushchev and he mentioned in his famous 'secret' speech of 1955 in which he denounced Stalin for had happened to the Kalmyks, and also the Chechens, the Ingush, the Balkars and the Karachai, but he made no reference to the Volga Germans or Crimean Tatars.

The cause of the Kalmyks had been raised by their compatriots in the United States and elsewhere. This had seen US Kalmyks attend the Bandung Conference in 1955 to help publicise the cause of their fellow countrymen exiled in Siberia. In the following year, 1956, Khrushchev reversed the deportation of the Kalmyks, and on 9 January 1957 the Presidium of the Supreme Soviet of the USSR issued another decree which announced 'the formation of the Kalmyk autonomous province in the structure of the Russian Soviet Federated Socialist Republic.' The Kalmyks were allowed to return home after thirteen years of exile. Many years later the writer Elza-

Bair Guchinova saw an old lady praying to a picture of Nikita Khrushchev. When asked why, she replied that Khrushchev had managed to achieve what the Gods had not. To her, he was a hero.

Formal rehabilitation, however, did not come until the *Law on the Rehabilitation of the Repressed Peoples* in 1991, and a speech made by Boris Yeltsin on 28 December 1993, when 28 December was made a day to remember the 'deported people'.

Rebuilding Kalmykia

The Kalmyks were overjoyed to return home. Many elderly people still have lights in their eyes as they describe the end of their exile. Some were Red Army veterans who risked their lives for the Soviet Union and tried to accept that their treatment was an aberration of Soviet policy. Most had lost family members and when they returned to their homes, some found other people living in them.

In 1949 there had been some exploratory drilling for oil but nothing much had eventuated although some oil was found in 1961. The new Soviet government quickly built large apartment blocks. Gradually as the government continued to expand, the old Red House was far too small and a much larger Government House was built in central Elista. In front of it there was a statue of Lenin, and the main street was now Lenin Street. The Rodina Cinema in Elista even appeared in a Soviet postage stamp in 1961 (right). The war hero, Bator Basanov, was the director of the Rodina Cinema from 1965 until his death in 1982.

On their return to Kalmykia, the Kalmyks started quickly to help preserve as much of their culture as they could. The Kalmyk Research and Development Bureau's institute of languages, literature and history which had been established on 1 June 1941, and then closed down eighteen months later, was reopened. Its first director, Ivan Kuznetsovich Ilishkin, had been teaching in Krasnoyarsk and then Kyrgyzstan, returned to be appointed to restart the public education system with Boris Pashkov becoming the second director.

Anatoly Kichikov who had been in the Military Aviation School in Grozny in 1942, and then deported to Siberia, had become an important figure in the public education system in Kazakhstan and Uzbekistan. He helped to set up the Kalmyk schools

and train more teachers with Leonid Kovalevich Sanzhinov taking over as headmaster of one of the schools in Elista.

Bemba Dzhimbinov was appointed secretary of the Communist Party Committee of Kalmykia and chairman of the Union of Writers of Kalmykia. He continued writing poetry; and Basang Byuryunovich Dordzhiyev helped to record many of the traditions of Kalmyk drama and theatre.

Sanji Kalyaevich Kalyaev, when he returned to Elista, became the deputy chief editor for the local newspaper and then from 1958 to 1960 was a senior research fellow at the Kalmyk Research Institute of Language, Literature and History, and also worked on teacher training courses becoming an Associate Professor of the Kalmyk language in 1961, editing a literary magazine and translating the plays of Molière into Kalmyk, being awarded the title of 'People's Poet of Kalmykia' in 1965.

During the period of the Soviet Union, Elista – indeed the whole of Kalmykia – was closed to tourists. Foreigners were allowed to go to Stalingrad, but no further south. What they did not see was that the Kalmyk people settled back in Kalmykia with relatively little animosity. In the 1960s and 1970s, and indeed during the 1980s, under Soviet rule, there was relative prosperity in the region. Food was plentiful and cheap, and many people admit that, in retrospect, they were very wasteful. The period of the Siberian exile was never forgotten, but time healed wounds. In Soviet Kalmykia, education was free and compulsory, and during this period, the vast majority of all people in Kalmykia became literate. Many books were published, and soon Elista

The war memorial in Elista commemorating those who died in conflicts after 1945. #

ПАМЯТИ ПОГИБШИХ ПРИ ИСПОЛНЕНИИ ВОИНСКОГО ДОЛГА

В РЕСПУБЛИКЕ АФГАНИСТАН

М С-Т	БУТКОВ Н.В.	1960	1980
РЯД	БАРАЕВ З.М.	1963	1982
РЯД	ХАДЫКИН А.Г.	1961	1982
РЯД	БУЛИНОВ Б.С.	1963	1982
РЯД	СЛИЗСКИЙ И.И.	1963	1982
РЯД	БУРАЕВ П.Н.	1963	1982
РЯД	ИЛЬИН А.Ю.	1963	1983
СЕРЖ	МАНДЖИЕВ В.М.	1964	1984
РЯД	ПЛОТНИКОВ Н.Б.	1964	1984
РЯД	ВАСИЛЕНКО В.А.	1966	1985
СЕРЖ	ДОРДЖИ-ГОРЯЕВ В.М.	1966	1985
РЯД	ГИРИН Р.П.	1967	1986
М.С-Т	ДОРЖИЕВ О.Б.	1967	1987
РЯД	ГРОМОВ С.В.	1967	1987
РЯД	БАБАЕВ Ю.И.	1967	1988

РЯД	ВДОВИКИН Г.В.	1976	1995
РЯД	ПУРНЕВ А.А.	1974	1995
РЯД	ДЬЯКОН Е.В.	1975	1995
РЯД	ПУГОВЕНКО А.С.	1975	1995
В-С	КУШАЕВ Е.Б.	1967	1995
РЯД	УБУШАЕВ Н.В.	1976	1996
РЯД	БАСАНГОВ М.Н.	1976	1996
М.С-Т	СКИБИН А.А.	1977	1996
РЯД	УБУШИЕВ С.Б.	1977	1996
РЯД	ЭРДНИЕВ Б.Э.	1977	1996
М-Р	АБДУЛИН В.М.	1952	1996
РЯД	РАКОВИЧ А.Е.	1974	1996
РЯД	КОВАЛЕНКО С.В.	1977	1996
РЯД	ЭРДНЕЕВ Б.О.	1980	1999
СТ.С-Т	ПАУПОВ З.А.	1980	2000

В ЧЕЧЕНСКОЙ РЕСПУБЛИКЕ

М.С-Т	ОНАЕВ Д.С.	1976	2000
РЯД	КУБРАКОВ А.Н.	1981	2000
РЯД	ВИННИКОВ А.Д.	1981	2000
РЯД	СВИНАРЕВ В.С.	1976	2000
РЯД	КАЧАНОВ А.Н.	1981	2000
СТ.С-Т	ОЧИРОВ А.В.	1966	2000
Л-НТ	ЕРМОЛОВ В.В.	1963	1995
РЯД	БЕМБЕЕВ А.Н.	1976	1996
СТ.ЛЛ	КУЛАГИН И.И.	1971	1996
СЕР	БУТКО В.В.	1973	1996
СТ.С-Т	ЭРДНЕЕВ С.Н.	1965	1996
СТ.Л-Т	БЕРКАСИНОВ Н.В.	1973	2000
РЯД	ХАЛЗРБЫНОВ В.Г.	1969	2001
П/П-К	ЕВСЕЕВ Ю.А.	1963	2001

М.С-Т	КОРНИКОВ С.Ю.	1981	2001
С-Т	ОЧИР-ГОРЯЕВ А.Г.	1980	2001
РЯД	АВДЖАЕВ Ч.В.	1983	2002
РЯД	ЧЕТЫРОВ О.И.	1977	1996
РЯД	ЛАРЛЫКОВ Г.Н.	1975	1995
РЯД	МУКУБЕНОВ С.А.	1980	2001
РЯД	БЮЛЯЕВ Б.С.	1982	2002
РЯД	ЧАЛАКОВ Б.В.	1983	2002
РЯД	МУКЛАЕВ В.Э.	1980	2002
РЯД	ХАНИНОВ А.А.	1983	2003
МЛ.Л-Т	МАНКАЕВ С.В.	1974	2007
М-Р	МАНКИРОВ К.Н.	1956	1995

boasted a range of newspapers. Health care was also free. And several Kalmyks started to achieve prominence in sports and chess. Kalmyks served in the Red Army, and fifteen young men from Elista died in Afghanistan.

In 1959 Kalmykia had celebrated 350th anniversary of 1609 – there were 64,882 Kalmyks in the census of the Soviet Union. It was muted especially given the high expectations that had followed from the celebrations of Dzanghar in 1940. But there was also for the first time for a long period, a celebration of several Kalmyks who had distinguished themselves during the Soviet Union. Colonel General Oka Ivanovich Gorodovikov who had been deputy commander of cavalry from 1943 until 1947 when he retired, had been made a Hero of the Soviet Union. He died on 26 February 1960 in Moscow, and eleven years later the town of Bashanta, some 240 kms west of Elista was renamed Gorodovikovsk in his honour.

The first high voltage electricity lines were installed in Kalmykia in 1962 and in the following year, Bosya Badmaevna Sangadzhieva, a writer of fiction, participated in the World Congress of Women, which was held in Moscow. In June 1967, the state library was named after Amur-Sanan; and on

The Amur-Sanan Library, Elista, 2013.#

Government House in Elista, 2011.#

5 November 1967 the first diesel locomotive trains appeared in Elista with the railway connection being extended in the following year, and the Kalmyk State University being founded in 1970 – with the statue of Lenin in the square between government hosue and the university being replaced with a new one sculpted by M. & O. Manigaran.

In 1971 Konstantin Erendzhenov a prominent writer and activist since the 1930s, was awarded the title of People's Poet of Kalmykia. Another cultural figure to be celebrated was the poet David Nikitich Kugultinov whose work was already acclaimed as a teenager. In 1941 he had joined the Red Army but this had not stopped him being deported to Siberia with the other Kalmyks. He had returned in 1957 and continued writing poetry winning a large number of Soviet literary awards and even having a minor planet named after him in 1975. David Kugultinov died on 17 June 2006.

The government of Kalmykia gained some autonomy, especially in the area of education. Kalmykia also elected members to the Supreme Soviet and to the Soviet Russian Congress of People's Deputies. The Kalmyk Art Gallery was

Young Pioneers marching around the statue of Lenin in its original position at the north end of the square in front of Government House in Elista during the 1970s.

Young Pioneers at the T-34 tank on the northern outskirts of Elista during the 1970s.

founded in 1977, and four years later, the local medical college was named after T. Khakhlinova. In 1983 the Pushkin Memorial in central Elista was designed by the sculptor Nikita Sandjiev.

However there were major changes afoot in the wider world. In 1989 the fall of the Berlin Wall signalled the start of the end of Communism in Eastern Europe. Mikhail Gorbachev had tried desperately to reform the Soviet Union and with inter-ethnic rioting in some parts of the Soviet Union – especially in Azerbaijan – Soviet hardliners staged an attempted coup to depose Gorbachev. This brought to power Boris Yeltsin. By the end of 1991, the Soviet Union had collapsed with Kalmykia remaining a part of the Russian Federation, now an independent country.

In September-October 1993, there was a constitutional crisis in Moscow, and Boris Yeltsin used a referendum he had held in April 1993, and won, as a mandate to dissolve the Supreme Soviet, and also the Soviet Russian Congress of People's Deputies, the Russian Parliament. At the height of the crisis, soldiers loyal to Yeltsin seized the television station as tens of thousands of Moscovites took to the streets to support the parliamentarians and oppose Yeltsin. Then Yeltsin sent in the army to attack the Russian Parliament on 4 October. Fighting resulted – which saw tanks supporting Yeltsin shelling the Parliament. During this crisis, a 31-year old Kalmyk politician, Kirsan Ilyumzhinov, managed to negotiate a ceasefire which allowed women and children to leave the parliament. Anywhere between two hundred and possibly as many as two thousand were killed. Boris Yeltsin was then in control of the Russian capital, and after pushing through a new Constitution, the country.

A stamp issued on 22 October 1970 to commemorate the 50th anniversary of the Kalmyk ASSR.

A stamp issued on 22 May 1980 commemorating *Dzanghar*.

Endza
(1813-1889)

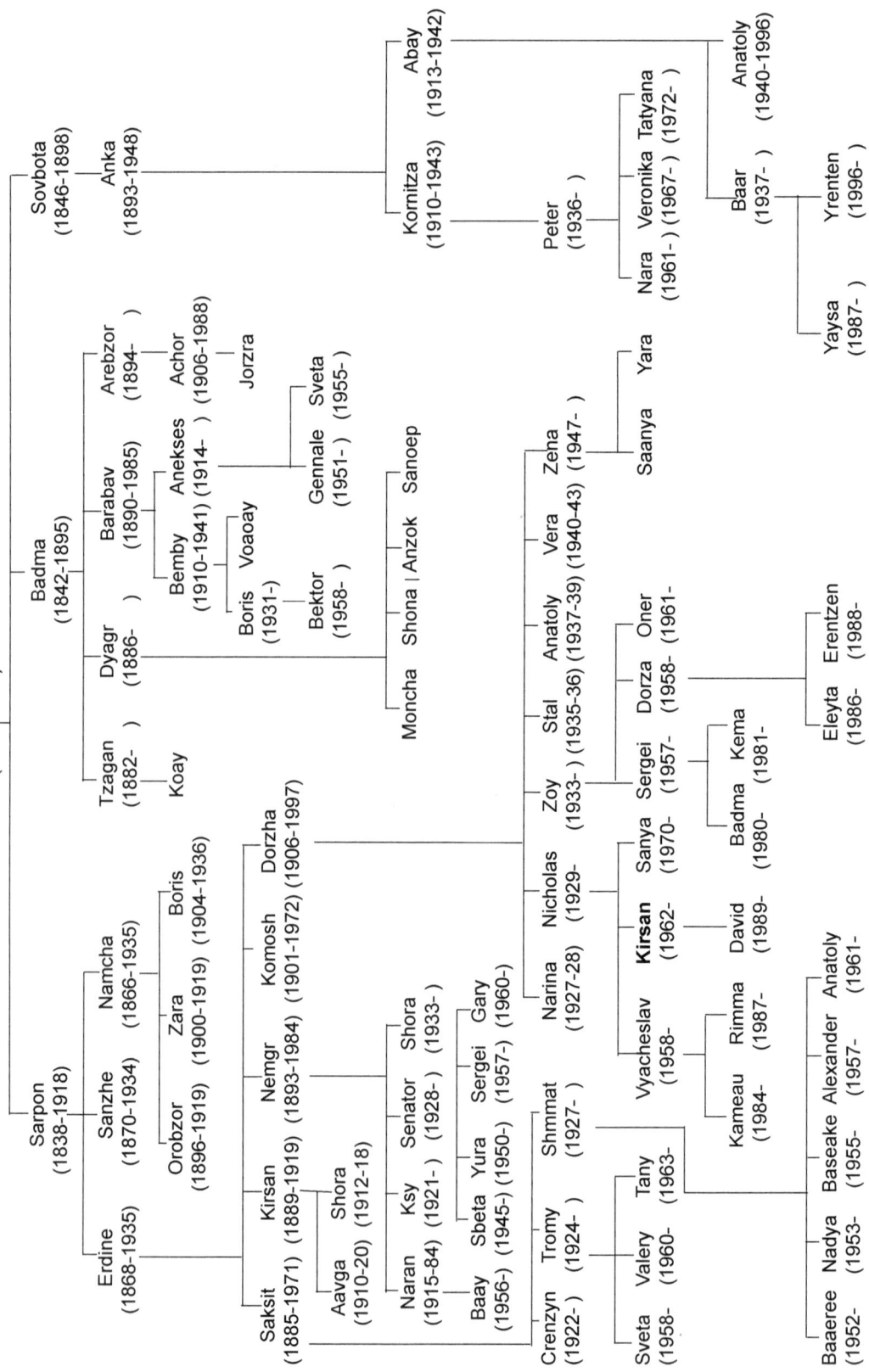

Sovbota
(1846-1898)

Badma
(1842-1895)

Sarpon
(1838-1918)

Anka
(1893-1948)

Abay
(1913-1942)

Anatoly
(1940-1996)

Kornitza
(1910-1943)

Baar
(1937-)

Peter
(1936-)

Nara
(1961-)

Veronika
(1967-)

Tatyana
(1972-)

Yrenten
(1996-)

Yaysa
(1987-)

Tzagan
(1882-)

Koay

Dyagr
(1886-)

Barabav
(1890-1985)

Arebzor
(1894-)

Achor
(1906-1988)

Anekses
(1914-)

Bemby
(1910-1941)

Voaoay

Jorzra

Boris
(1931-)

Gennale
(1951-)

Sveta
(1955-)

Bektor
(1958-)

Moncha   Shona   Anzok   Sanoep

Vera

Zena
(1947-)

Saanya

Yara

Anatoly
(1937-39)

Stal
(1935-36)

Zoy
(1933-)

Dorza
(1958-)

Oner
(1961-)

Sergei
(1957-)

Badma
(1980-)

Kema
(1981-)

Eleyta
(1986-

Erentzen
(1988-

Nicholas
(1929-

Sanya
(1970-)

David
(1989-)

Rimma
(1987-)

Kameau
(1984-)

Kirsan
(1962-)

Vyacheslav
(1958-

Narina
(1927-28)

Erdine
(1868-1935)

Sanzhe
(1870-1934)

Namcha
(1866-1935)

Orobzor
(1896-1919)

Zara
(1900-1919)

Boris
(1904-1936)

Saksit
(1885-1971)

Kirsan
(1889-1919)

Nemgr
(1893-1984)

Komosh
(1901-1972)

Dorzha
(1906-1997)

Aavga
(1910-20)

Shora
(1912-18)

Naran
(1915-84)

Ksy
(1921-)

Senator
(1928-)

Shora

Gary
(1960-)

Sergei
(1957-)

Yura
(1950-)

Sbeta
(1945-)

Baay
(1956-)

Crenzyn
(1922-)

Tromy
(1924-)

Shmmat
(1927-)

Tany
(1963-

Valery
(1960-

Sveta
(1958-

Baseake
(1955-

Alexander
(1957-

Anatoly
(1961-

Nadya
(1953-

Baaeree
(1952-

4.
Kirsan Ilyumzhinov, Chess and the Emergence of Modern Kalmykia

In April, six months before the Constitutional Crisis which brought Boris Yeltsin to power, Kirsan Ilyumzhinov, a former Kalmykian chess prodigy, became the first elected president of Kalmykia.

Kirsan Nicolayevich Ilyumzhinov had been born at 5.56 am on 5 April 1962, in Elista. He was the second son of Nicholas and Rimma Ilyumzhinov; they already had a son, Vyacheslav, born in 1958. The details are recorded in Kirsan Ilyumzhinov's autobiography. At birth he weighed 3.8 kilos. It was the Year of the Tiger – and an early birth meant that the child had the day ahead of him. By tradition, this signals somebody who would rise early and have the full day to accomplish his dreams. The tiger was, of course, a symbol of the powerful 'Lord of the Jungle'. In China, the tiger combines beauty, strength and energy. The tiger also serves to protect people from fire, theft and evil spirits.

The family had some debate over what to call the new child. Just before his mother went into labour, his father's brother, Kirsan Ilyumzhinov came to the family home. He had been a war hero during the Second World War. During the period of Stalin's rule in the late 1940s and early 1950s, when the Kalmyk people were deported to Siberia, the two brothers had lost touch with each other. They had both survived and were now reunited, with the baby imminent. Nicholas Ilyumzhinov planned to call the baby Kirsan after the brother he had not seen for so long. And Nicholas's own uncle was also called Kirsan Ilyumzhinov, and he had been a hero in the Russian Civil War.

This original Kirsan Ilyumzhinov (1889–1919) had served in the Russian Imperial Army during World War I. Then after the Russian Revolution, he had been one of the few Kalmyks who served in the Red Army in Belorussia (modern-day Belarus) and then in the Ukraine during the Russian Civil War. He had fought the White Russians and died during the conflict, leaving a widow and a ten year-old son – the boy dying in the following year. His family were told that he shot himself but gradually news reached them that he had done so when faced with a terrible dilemma. When the White Russian army of General Deniken retreated to Kolkata in the Crimea, they tried to escape from Russia. The Red Army unit which included the thirty-

Namcha Ilyumzhinov (1866–1935) and others.

Sanzhe Ilyumzhinov (1870–1934) and a colleague.

Kirsan Ilyumzhinov (1889–1919).

The author with Nicholas Ilyumzhinov, Elista, 2011.

year-old Kirsan Ilyumzhinov caught up with them. Following orders from Leon Trotsky and other hardline Communists, the Red Army had orders to kill all the Whites they captured. The group which Ilyumzhinov captured included Kalmyks as well as Cossacks, and there were many old people as well as women and children. Kirsan Ilyumzhinov refused orders to kill these stating that he could not live with himself if he committed such an atrocity, and committed suicide. It is one of those tragic stories emerging from the Russian Civil War and has some similarities with Jan Józef Szczepański's story *Buty* ('Boots') published in 1947 in which, at the end of World War II, a Polish partisan unit is ordered to execute captured Kalmyks.

Thus with Nicholas's uncle and brother both called Kirsan, there were two reasons to call the baby Kirsan, which means 'Golden Light'. However life is never that simple. There was also a grandmother around to give advice on the birth. Sulda Badmamovna had just had a dream that concerned her own father, Badma, and she decided that her grandson should be named after him – Badma means 'Lotus', and this is now the official symbol of Kalmykia. An argument started between Nicholas Ilyumzhinov and his mother-in-law – the baby was registered at birth as Kirsan. But there were still problems in store. With both his parents at work – his father was an engineer and his mother a vet – the grandmother helped bring up the boy and always called him Badma. It was not until he started school that the boy even realised that his real name was actually Kirsan.

As well as a great-uncle who served in the Civil War, Kirsan's grandfather had been a war hero from the Red Army during World War II, and several other family members served in the military. However all of this had not stopped the family being deported to Siberia. Nicholas Ilyumzhinov was twenty when the Kalmyks were deported from Elista. He had taken care of his mother and little sister – his father having been fighting the Germans at the time. They protested the military credentials of their family with a number of them still serving in the Red Army but they were all deported to Siberia. There Nicholas Ilyumzhinov learnt from his own grandfather about the history of Kalmyks and of Kalmykia but it was not until thirty-three when he finally returned to Elista. Fifty-five years later, he still had tears in his eyes as he spoke of this return and the restoration of political rights for all the Kalmyks. The first years back at Elista were very difficult as the families tried to get themselves together again.

The Ilyumzhinov family in 1962, and (below) the young Kirsan Ilyumzhinov.

Only two years after the return, Nicholas Ilyumzhinov and Rimma (née Sergeevna) had their first son, Vyacheslav. And four years later, Kirsan was born. At kindergarten, by his own description, Kirsan had a slightly larrikin streak in him, and even claimed that he smoked his first cigarette. Involved in fights with other small boys, he was obviously an energetic young boy. Indeed Munro-Butler-Johnstone had remarked in 1875, 'The Kalmuck children are precocious and sharp in the extreme'.

At home, the Ilyumzhinovs lived in a traditional middle class Soviet household. Both parents worked. There was some music – Nicholas Ilyumzhinov liked Chopin, Bach and Tchaikovsky; he disliked twentieth century composers. But much of the family's spare time was taken up with reading. Nicholas Ilyumzhinov was passionate about Pushkin, but also liked Tolstoy, Dostoyevsky, Tchekhov and also the works of Mikhail Lermantov, styled 'the poet of the Caucasus'. Lermantov had been born near Tula, just north of Kalmykia, but fell ill as a youngster so his parents took him to the Caucasus where, in later life, he served as an officer in the Dragoons. However Nicholas's favourite author

Nicholas and Rimma Ilyumzhinov

was Mikhail Sholokhov whose famous book *And Quiet Flows the Don* had been published in serialised form between 1928 and 1940.

There were few schools in Elista, and the young Kirsan did not go to school until he was about six years old. As he set off for school on his first day, his parents told him to behave himself. His brother, four years his senior, was already at the same school. Vyacheslav was a model student – serious, hard-working and completed all his homework on time. On that first day, Kirsan accompanied his brother to School No 3. Kirsan later wrote that the school was nicknamed 'the children's home' as most of the children of the prominent Kalmyks sent their children there. Located in the centre of the town, the young Kirsan went down the tree-lined street, through the gateway and across the courtyard, climbing the five steps and then passing through the double doors into the school building. After finding his classroom, his teacher, Yelena Alekseyevna, called the roll and the young Kirsan – who still thought his name was Badma – did not answer his name.

Gradually Kirsan Ilyumzhinov came to like the school and emerged as an avid reader. He had some problems settling down but this is understandable. He was occasionally truant, and in his memoirs he noted that he smoked. Not only his family, but those of all other Kalmyks had been through an immense trauma – personal and collective. They had been displaced, lost families, and had only just returned to their native city to find it occupied by non-Kalmyks, and themselves essentially initially treated as foreigners in their own land. Some Kalmyk accounts, especially poems, speak of this sense of alienation that many felt in that period.

Kirsan Ilyumzhinov's old school is now the Kalmykia Lyceum, with School No 3 taking over a newer 1960s building in another part of Elista. In the new School No 3 there is a museum which preserves the school books of Kirsan Ilyumzhinov, along with his red scarf and blue shorts from his days as a Young Pioneer. Cherishing his schooldays, he regularly goes back to his old school (in its new location) and talks to the students.

Kirsan Ilyumzhinov's school, now the Kalmykia Lyceum, 2011.

In his autobiography, *The Crown of Thorns*, Kirsan Ilyumzhinov makes much of the pranks he played as a school boy. For many people reflecting on their school days, that is certainly what they remember. Kirsan Ilyumzhinov certainly described himself as a bit of an indifferent scholar but many others remember him differently. His father described him as an excellent student with very good grades, and the surviving school mark books in the museum in School No 3 support this, as does testimony from others at his school at the same time. Certainly he would have needed to achieve high marks to get his place at university in Moscow. At the school he also saw how children of Communist Party leaders were treated better than others, and their misdemeanours often overlooked. When he complained about this, he sometimes found himself in trouble.

Kirsan Ilyumzhinov at school

At home, it was young Kirsan's paternal grandfather who taught him to play draughts and then moved onto chess which soon became his passion. Kirsan later wrote:

> I became fascinated by chess; I would sit at the checker-board for hours forgetting everything. My ardent and unrestrained imagination as a child, influenced by the movies I had seen and the books I had read about outstanding men, all became oddly mixed up with my love of chess. The thirty-two white and thirty-two black checks on the board seemed to me to encompass the duality of the whole world. My love for chess has remained with me until this very day.
>
> A Buddhist legend has it that two residents of heaven once descended to earth and started to play chess in the middle of the boundless steppe. They were approached by a very young fellow who was grazing a flock of sheep. He began to watch the game. When the game was over the Gods disappeared. When the herdsman looked back he saw that his clothes had been reduced to ashes, his whip had crumbled from old age, and he himself had become a decrepit old man. People say that chess was invented by the Gods.

Vyacheslav Ilyumzhinov.

The young boy's interest in chess came around the time he fell very ill and had to convalesce in a sanatorium in the town of Yessentuki, near Stavropol. There he soon helped look after some of the other patients, and it was not long before he returned to Elista, and to chess.

Kirsan's father and his older brother both played chess but his father later confessed that he was 'not crazy about it'. When he was only six, Kirsan started winning games against boys twice his age. The young Kirsan quickly understood that chess teaches patience, caution and planning ahead. At around

The museum in the new School No 3 in 2009 (above), #; and in 2013 (below).#

that this his father stopped playing against his sons as they could both easily beat him.

There were starting to be changes in Soviet society. Imported clothes began to appear, and new found confidence during the Brezhnev years saw more and better food being available in the shops, without people realising that the economy was actually stagnating. It was also now possible to listen to the British BBC news and Voice of America with few problems. Kirsan Ilyumzhinov's father was working at the Department of Industry of the City Party Committee, and his mother was still a vet. It remained a happy middle class Soviet family, with Nicholas Ilyumzhinov developing a great passion for local history and also in military history with regular memorial services to commemorate those killed during World War II.

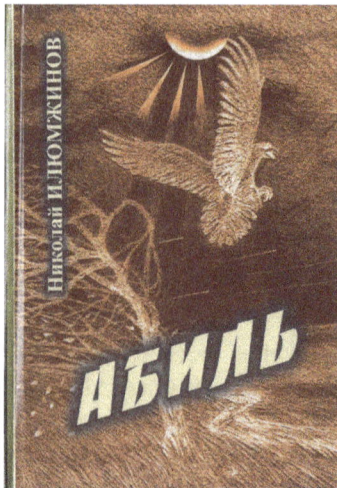

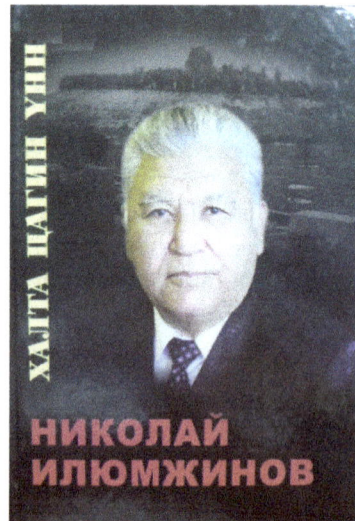

Books written by Nicholas Ilyumzhinov.

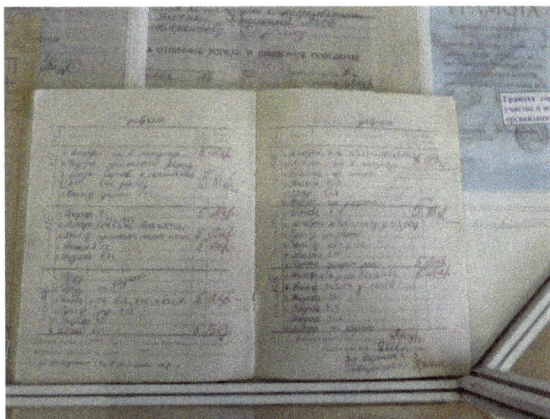

However Kirsan began to notice a difference between the history his father related, and that taught at school. His father was passionate about Kalmyk history and the folk stories which had been handed down from one generation to another. By contrast the history which formed part of the school curriculum made no mention of the Kalmyks. Kirsan queried why there was no mention of Prince Tyumen who led the Kalmyks into Paris in 1814 – the answer from his teacher was unsatisfactory. The only aspect of Kalmyk history and culture which was undergoing a revival was the Dzanghar epic which fascinated the young Kirsan, and also all young Kalmyks.

Kirsan Ilyumzhinov was ten when he was selected to take part in a chess championship for the Kalmyk Republic being held at Togliatti. The team from School No 3 won. He was soon going to other tournaments in nearby parts of the Soviet Union. As well as improving his chess, he steadily became more self-reliant. He later wrote that with travelling around, he had to do his own washing, sewing on missing buttons, ironing shirts and even darning. By the age of twelve, he was keen to locate bargains, and often bought the family food from the people working in collectives rather than going to the market or the shops. Over these years Kirsan also had to help his family in routine chores – his parents having another son, Sanal, born in 1970. He helped bathe his brother and wash up, as his parents were out at work.

A member of the Young Pioneers, in October 1977 Kirsan visited Leningrad (St Petersburg) just prior to winning the chess championship. In October 1977 the city was bedecked with flags to celebrate the 60th anniversary of the Russian Revolution. He visited the *Aurora* and other sites connected with the revolution. However he was always conscious that many people in other parts of the Soviet Union knew nothing about the Kalmyks.

Kirsan Ilyumzhinov with other members of the Young Pioneers (above); and his uniform (below).#

Then, in 1978, Kirsan surprised his family, his school and indeed the region when he won the state's chess championship and became the chess champion of the Kalmyk Republic.

Chess in Kalmykia

The oldest surviving chess pieces in the world – dating back to the second century AD – were discovered in Uzbekistan in 1973, and it seems likely that chess may have originated in Central Asia. Chess was popular with many European nobles with its history in Central Asia being less documented. Certainly by the eighteenth century chess playing seems to have been common among many Kalmyks. What seems to be the earliest western account of Kalmyks playing chess is by the British diplomat George Bogle. Born in Scotland in 1746, the son of a merchant, Bogle was the youngest of nine children and he decided to leave Scotland to try to make his fortune in British India. There he worked for Warren Hastings and in 1774 went on a British mission to Tibet. He and his companion Alexander Hamilton were the first Britons ever to enter Tibet. There he met with Kalmyk merchants and played chess with them. In his account,

> The arrival of a large party of Kalmuks (sic) furnished me with enough of combatants. Their method of playing differs from ours, in the privilege of moving two steps being confined to the first pawn played by each

Х. Косиев — 1935 г.   Д. Сангаджиев — 1938 г.   Л. Дамбинов — 1939-40 гг.

З. Долгинов   К. Илюмжинов — 1978 г.   А. Кариков

А. Утнасунов 1999, 2002, 2005 гг.   В. Поддубный   2001 г.   Э. Инаркиев   2003 г.

Some of the chess champions of Kalmykia with Kirsan Ilyumzhinov in the centre, Chess Academy, Elista, 2011.#

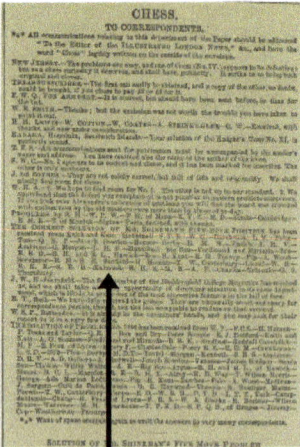

A chess player using the name 'Kalmuck', solving a chess problem. *The Illustrated London News* (9 November 1872).

The young Kirsan Ilyumzhinov playing chess.

party; in castling and stalemate being unknown; and in the game being reckoned equal when the king is left solus without a piece or a pawn on the board.

It is a generous principle. In my first trials of skill with the Tatars, I used often to come off loser. For when a Siberian sits down to chess, he gets two or three of his countrymen to assist him ; they lay all their great bare heads together canvassing and consulting about every move. At length I found out the way of managing them, and encountered them with their own weapons. If I could not get a Siberian to enter the lists with me in single combat, I engaged an equal number of Tatars on my side, and we used to beat them hollow.

And Bogle's experiences were not unique. Peter Simon Pallas and Benjamin Bergmann who were in Kalmykia later than Bogle, noted that chess was much played by the Buddhist clergy in Kalmykia. J C Hallman, in his book, *The Chess Artist*, notes the tradition that a rich Kalmyk brought an ivory chess set to Kalmykia and donated it to a temple in 1860. This may have led to a revival in interest in chess coming ninety years after Bogle's account. Although it will never be known with any certainly who introduced chess into Kalmykia, it to have been played by many people in the late eighteenth and nineteenth centuries.

By the late nineteenth century, chess was a favoured pastime in many parts of the world, and especially in Russia. There were soon professional players who made their money attending tournaments, with many also teaching chess at schools and in clubs. In 1914 Tsar Nicholas II had held a chess championship at St. Petersburg where, according to tradition, the five best players were given the title of 'grandmaster', one that is still awarded for the best players in the world. Three years later, Lenin, whose grandmother was Kalmyk (see p. 44, 72), came to power. He was also a keen player although after the Revolution he had much less time for recreations.

Under Stalin whilst there were so many restrictions on what people could do, chess was openly encouraged. School tournaments and local chess clubs flourished. The world chess champion from 1927 until his death in 1946, Alexander Alekhine, was also a Russian, albeit a White Russian exile. Since fleeing the country in 1921, Alekhine had not been able to return, although his great adversary (and predecessor as world chess champion), José Raul Capablanca, had travelled to

128

Moscow in 1936, and played the best Russian players.

By the late 1930s a Soviet citizen, Mikhail Botvinnik was emerging as one of the best players in the world, and in 1948 was given the accolade as the World Chess Champion after two rounds of games held in The Hague and Moscow. And four of the five who vied with Bovinnik for the title had all been born in Russia. The runner-up was Vasily Smyslov from Moscow. Drawing in third place was Paul Keres, born in Estonia when it was still a part of the Russian Empire (and by 1948 a Soviet citizen), and Samuel Reshevsky, who was a US citizen but who had been born in Russian Poland, although the borders had since been redrawn. The only other competitor, Max Euwe, briefly a world chess champion, was from the Netherlands.

This predominance of Soviet citizens at the top of the international chess scene continued with Botvinnik being succeeded as World Chess Champion by Smyslov in 1957, winning back his 'crown' in 1958, and then losing it to another Soviet citizen, Mikhail Tal, from Latvia. Tal certainly visited Elista to play chess, and the others may well have done so.

Botvinnik made a come-back in 1961, then Tigran Petrosian from Tiflis, Georgia – also then a part of the Soviet Union and only 518 kms from Elista – held the title from 1963 until 1969, whereupon Boris Spassky, from Leningrad, became World Chess Champion. However there was a shock throughout the Soviet Union when the World Championship was held in Reykjavik in 1972 and Spassky was defeated by an American, Bobby Fischer. Fischer's mother was from Russia (and his father from Germany); and his parents had been married in

Exhibits in the Chess City Museum, Elista, from the collection of Mikhail Taal.#

129

Moscow, with his pregnant mother going to the United States – Bobby being born in Illinois. In spite of his Russian heritage, the outcome was hailed in the USA as much as it was mourned in the Soviet Union – the match seeming to epitomise the clash between the two countries in the Cold War.

Kalmykian state chess championships had been held from at least 1935 until 1940, and then were not held again until 1957. In 1978 when Kirsan Ilyumzhinov won the chess championship for Kalmykia, a Russian was again the world chess champion. Probably the most generous description of Bobby Fischer was that he was 'eccentric'. He was self-centred, petulant and arrogant. Many Americans began to be shocked when they heard of his behaviour outside tournaments, and even during them – except for his time actually playing a game. He had won the World Chess Championship as much by wearing down Spassky as actually defeating him on the chessboard. And Fischer was eager not to lose his title so refused to play the challenger, Anatoly Karpov.

In 1975 with Fischer's refusal, he had been stripped of his title and Karpov was now the World Chess Champion. Born in Zlatoust, a small town in the Urals, Karpov had started to play when he was four, and it was only a few days before his 24th birthday, that had become the world chess champion inspiring many Soviet, and indeed other young people around the world.

Chess Champion of Kalmykia

With such encouragement in the Soviet media for the playing of chess, it did not take long for the young Kirsan to continue to improve his chess skills. As a boy, according to his own memoirs, Kirsan was often slightly unruly. The isolation of Elista as well as the huge dislocation in Kalmyk society only two decades earlier clearly had an effect on children growing up in Kalmykia in the 1960s and 1970s. Whilst the Communist Party had pledged itself to offer certainty to the people of the Soviet Union, Kalmykia had been invaded and the Kalmyks had been deported to Siberia, and remained alienated in many ways from mainstream Soviet society.

In 1978, at the age of fourteen, when Kirsan Ilyumzhinov won the Kalmykian chess championship, he became famous throughout Kalmykia. Yelena Pokaninova, the same age as him, of mixed Kalmyk-French ancestry, attended School No 4 and when she heard of his victory after reading about the win in the local newspapers, she and her friends flocked over to School No 3 to see Kirsan who was now a local celebrity. Kirsan

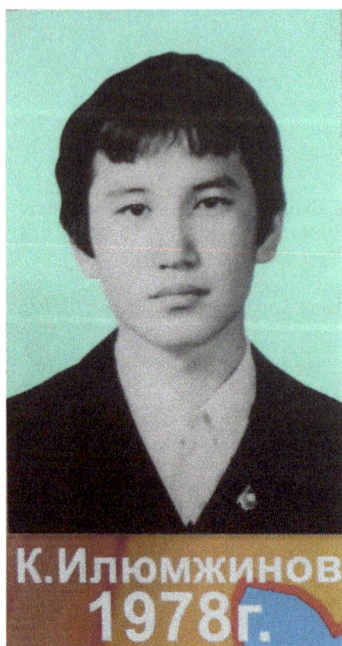

К.Илюмжинов
1978г.

Ilyumzhinov was briefly overwhelmed by this and he tried to avoid the limelight. Some months later Yelena met him at a Young Pioneers' Camp and congratulated him on his victory. Quietly spoken, he accepted her thanks, still overwhelmed by his new-found fame.

Although Kirsan could have continued playing competitive chess, he instead decided to stop playing regularly, and became a minor figure on the Soviet chess scene until November 1995 when he was elected President of FIDE, the International Chess Federation, and set about associating chess with Kalmykia, and Kalmykia with chess.

What stopped Kirsan playing chess as a youth was the emerging teenage scene in the Soviet Union. Kirsan enjoyed music. His father had bought a record player soon after coming back to Elista, and the teenage Kirsan had built up a large record collection with many of his friends coming over where they could listen to jazz, initially to the disdain of his father. Then after leaving school Kirsan Ilyumzhinov faced an interesting dilemma. With compulsory national service in the Soviet Union, he did not receive his call-up papers. He had to decide whether this was a temporary oversight – and would be noticed quickly and he would receive his call-up notice, possibly in the following year; or whether he would be able to escape national service altogether. The teenage Kirsan decided that the best course of action was to alert the authorities. This would prevent him being called up in the following year and having to serve alongside younger boys, rather than with his school friends.

National service in the Soviet Union was tough and rough. Kirsan Ilyumzhinov found it extremely trying, in spite of being a keen boxer. He later wrote:

> The Kalmyks say: 'When the strong exert themselves they grow even stronger, but when the weak do the same they break their backs. If you did not buckle in the army, then you were ready for civilian life where the same laws govern. In that sense the army is a great school of survival. I survived it. I built up strong muscles and learned a great deal in the army which prepared me for life under socialism.

Business and Politics

After completing his national service, Kirsan then worked as a mechanic and fitter at the Zveda plant in Elista. His brother had trained as a diplomat and Kirsan soon developed an interest in politics. The tensions of the Cold War had reached a new height with the election of Ronald Reagan as the US president. The Americans soon realised that the Soviet Union was facing major economic problems and sought to win the Cold War by waging

Kirsan Ilyumzhinov (left) during National Service.

Kirsan Ilyumzhinov.

an economic war against their foe. However with massive natural resources, the Soviet Union remained complacent to this threat.

During this period, only some parts of Kalmyk history were celebrated. The stories of Lenin's grandmother and Colonel General Gorodovikov grew in importance. Indeed on 22 April each year Young Pioneers from Kalmykia brought flowers to the tomb of Lenin. The local media also started to mention the role of some Kalmyks who supported the rebels during the Pugachev Revolt of 1773–75. Other areas, however, continued to remain off limits, but the Soviet Union was changing.

Being able to learn languages easily, and with less discrimination against Kalmyks, and a recognition that many of them, including members of Kirsan's own family, had fought in the Red Army, Kirsan was able to get a place at the prestigious Moscow Institute of International Relations where he studied from 1983 until 1989. This saw him move to the Soviet capital during a period of major changes that were to follow the death of Leonid Brezhnev in 1982. At the Institute of International Relations, Kirsan met children and grandchildren of the Communist Party leaders. As Kirsan wrote:

> Many behaved obsequiously and literally danced attendance on them, trying to make friends with the scions of powerful families who were 'doomed' to getting the most enviable job placements. As a matter of fact, quite a few among the patricians were rather decent and likeable fellows; they had their faults and flaws (but who doesn't?) and their strong and weak points.

In his studies, it was necessary to focus heavily on the works of Karl Marx, Friedrich Engels, and also Vladimir Lenin. Kirsan Ilyumzhinov began to think more deeply about them and not only see what they had wanted to achieve in societal changes, but also where they had gone wrong. Being at the Moscow Institute of International Relations, he also had access to foreign media which allowed him to find out about other countries. He also became fascinated by UFOs with sightings leading to a publishing boom in the Soviet Union as well as elsewhere in the world.

One of Kirsan's friends at the Institute was the son of Babrak Karmal, the pro-Soviet leader of Afghanistan. Mixing with a number of other Afghans and some Iranians, Kirsan soon found himself the subject of the attention of the feared KGB. He was even brought in for questioning about his mixing with foreigners. The interrogators thought that as a Kalmyk, Kirsan might harbour grudges about the deportation of the Kalmyks in 1943 but this was not the case. The KGB quickly released Kirsan who headed back to his studies.

On his completion of his degree, Kirsan Ilyumzhinov then went into business as the sales manager of the Soviet-Japanese joint venture company Liko-Raduga in Moscow. This was involved in the selling of Audi and Volkswagen cars, and also had a separate involvement in the trade in cattle skins, manufacturing agricultural produce, and running restaurants in Moscow and Japan. The market economy was beginning to impact on the Soviet Union and Kirsan soon found himself being paid $5,000 a month – the average *annual* income in the country at that time was $7,800. There were also soon performance-related bonuses. Operating with Liko-Raduga, the company was keen to invest in a wide range of projects. Kirsan described later how he often worked until 3 am. His business skills developed and from 1990–93 he was the President of the SAN Corporation in Moscow. It was during this time that Kirsan Ilyumzhinov became very wealthy as the company expanded to become involved in a wide range of joint-ventures. His foray into business coincided with the collapse of the Soviet Union and there were great fortunes to be made with the privatisation of many old Soviet companies. Some of these ventures were very successful, but others saw investors incur large losses.

Returning to Elista in the winter of 1990, Kirsan arranged for the purchase of grain and wool from Kalmykia. The wool was now able to be sold overseas, and Kirsan increased his fortune. And Elista was undergoing change with a revival of interest in Kalmyk history. Since World War II, Kalmykia had been closed to foreign visitors, and there had been no mention of the region in foreign guidebooks of the period. Now restrictions were lifted. Many overseas Kalmyks had been able to visit Kalmykia for the first time from 1989. Some families which had been divided since World War II were able to be reunited, or learnt about what had happened to family members. In 1990 the first Kalmyk Congress since World War II was convened in Elista, and delegates from the overseas 'White Bone' aristocracy were allowed to attend. There were some calls for independence but these did not predominate. Beyond the nationalist emotions, it was clear that Kalmykia could never survive as an independent country. Kirsan wrote:

> Later, when in the West, meeting up with Kalmyk émigrés, I would hear their terrible stories, feel their pain, and admire the purity of these people's hearts. It was they who … after the war was over, came out against exiling the Kalmyks, collected signatures, wrote petitions and

Kalmykia celebrated on a Russian stamp, 25 May 2000.

133

Elista in the 1970s with the statue of Lenin at the north end of the square between Government House and the new Kalmyk State University.

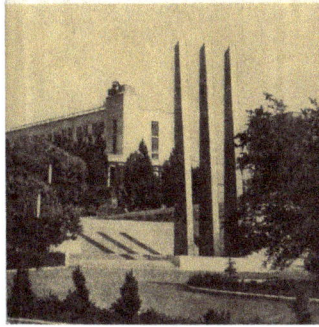

КАЛМЫКИЯ

Д. Б. Пюрвеев
АРХИТЕКТУРА КАЛМЫКИИ

КАЛМЫЦКАЯ АССР ЗА 50 ЛЕТ СОВЕТСКОЙ ВЛАСТИ

A range of books published about Kalmykia during the 1960s, 1970s and early 1980s.

Б. Б. ГОРОДОВИКОВ
СОВЕТСКАЯ КАЛМЫКИЯ НА ПОДЪЕМЕ

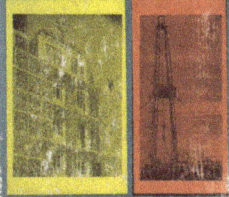

С. В. МАНДЖИЕВ Н. В. КЛЮКИН
КАЛМЫЦКАЯ АССР

В годы суровых испытаний

И. М. МАЦАКОВ
КАЛМЫЦКАЯ СОВЕТСКАЯ ХУДОЖЕСТ- ВЕННАЯ ЛИТЕРАТУРА
1920-1930

Элдя Кектеев
ИСТОКИ ЛЮБВИ
СТИХИ ПОЭМЫ

А. И. КУКИШ
животный мир калмыкии
ПТИЦЫ

А. И. Близнюк, Л. Н. Любаев, В. Н. Любаев
животный мир калмыкии
МЛЕКОПИТАЮЩИЕ

БАДМИН АЛЕКСЕЙ
РЕВДОЛЬГАН

А. Г. Митиров
ОЙРАТЫ- КАЛМЫКИ: ВЕКА И ПОКОЛЕНИЯ

АЛЕКСЕЙ БАДМАЕВ
СТРАНА БУМБА

Kirsan Ilyumzhinov and his mother.

turned for support to the United Nations Organization, heads of state and prominent churchmen. It was they who first raised the issue of allowing Kalmyks to return to their native land; who rang the bells and cried out to the world public, thus forcing Khrushchev to allow them to come back home after thirteen years in exile.

Entering politics

When Kirsan returned to Elista in 1990, he found that there were elections for the People's Deputies who would represent Kalmykia in Moscow. The elections were expected to be, as they had been since the 1920s, a formality. Friends suggested to Kirsan that he should stand. Before making up his mind, he contacted his older brother who was in Mongolia at the time. Vyacheslav Ilyumzhinov, forever the diplomat, suggested that Kirsan should not stand because it would attract all sorts of unwanted attention.

However Kirsan Ilyumzhinov decided, however, that he would stand and as his brother had predicted, attacks on him started to appear in newspapers. Contesting the election caused Kirsan to travel far more widely in Kalmykia than he had ever done before. Outside Elista, he found much more poverty than he had expected, but also there was hope that a new leadership might be able to change the state. Kirsan Ilyumzhinov was easily elected and when he returned to Moscow as a member of the Chamber of People's Deputies, he became involved in lobbying on behalf of Kalmyks, and also Kalmykia in general.

It was a period of great constitutional turmoil. The Belovezhskaya Pushcha Conference confirmed that the constituent republics of the USSR did have the right to self-determination. There still remained a query whether or not autonomous and semi-autonomous regions such as Kalmykia also had the same rights of secession. Fighting started in some places as one ethnic group turned on another, and on 26 December 1992 the Supreme Soviet finally confirmed the dissolution of the Soviet Union. And it was not long before people in some parts of the Russian Federation considered independence. In Kalmykia there was soon a power struggle which reflected the problems in Moscow.

Presidential Elections in Kalmykia

In early 1993 plans were drawn up by which the presidents of the various republics in Russia would be elected by the people of that republic. These presidents had powers similar to that of governors of US states, and to make them directly elected was

a move to decentralise power in Russia and was profoundly to change the country, for the most part, for the better.

With elections in Kalmykia imminent, the Communists were keen to hold onto office, and there were also liberals anxious to take power from them. Kirsan Ilyumzhinov decided to stand as a third party candidate – an independent. He was, by this time, wealthy, and became famous for his campaign slogan that a wealthy president would be a safeguard against corruption. He undertook that if he was elected, he would draw no salary. More importantly, he promised a new government – a younger government untainted by the Communist era. He also promised that his election would lead to freedom of worship and also prosperity.

Importing a nine-metre long Lincoln Continental car to Elista, Kirsan used it to drive around the city, and out to the countryside where the majority of Kalmykians lived. He visited farms, villages and herding stations. Elections in the Soviet Union had been fairly lacklustre affairs, and initially few people outside Kalmykia paid any attention to what was happening as Kirsan Ilyumzhinov and his supporters toured the state. His election team consisted largely of his friends from school and university. They were the people he knew and trusted, and he was always loyal to those who had been loyal to him.

Standing against him was General Ochirov who had created a reputation during political infighting in nearby Chechnya, and the general was expected to win. With more newspapers in Kalmykia, the press launched attacks on Kirsan and an audit team even arrived in Elista to try to find some compromising details about his new-found wealth. But as well as problems in Kalmykia, there were also many changes afoot in Moscow. Boris Yeltsin who had championed these democratic reforms was now under attack himself. Kirsan had to break off his campaigning to help shore up the numbers for Yeltsin in the parliament. And whilst in Moscow, Kirsan's businesses were again subjected to another audit. Once again, nothing irregular was discovered.

The elections were held and on the evening of 12 April 1993, when the votes were tallied in Elista, to everyone's great surprise, Kirsan Ilyumzhinov had managed to win – he had managed to get 65% of the vote. He and his supporters at their campaign headquarters celebrated into the night. The Communists in Government House who expected to win were holding their own party, of sorts, when news arrived that they had lost. In the morning after the election victory, Kirsan Ilyumzhinov and his supporters turned up at Government House to take over. To

Kirsan Ilyumzhinov taking the oath of office.

their shock they found that the Communists had trashed much of the building, having smashed many windows and broken the furniture. The Communists had finally found out that the people of Kalmykia actually disliked them and were none too pleased with this discovery. And not only had the carpets and office furniture been stolen, but the bank accounts of the government ministries were empty and large numbers of government possessions had either been sold cheaply by the outgoing government to fellow Communists, or had simply 'disappeared'.

President of Kalmykia

Kirsan Ilyumzhinov was sworn in as President amidst jubilation in Elista as people had voted for change. Many years later some still talk of him as being a 'young face' compared to the older candidates standing against him who were clearly against change. President Kirsan Ilyumzhinov, as he was now, gathered his closest advisers around him at Government House, and he issued his first presidential order – for his staff to get pens and paper – and then they got down to planning the transformation of Kalmykia. His first aim was to streamline the government of the state. With a population of about 320,000, there were 130 deputies for the local Kalmykian parliament. There were also forty government ministries. Kirsan reduced the number of deputies to 25, and amalgamated the ministries into four – later adding a fifth ministry for religious affairs. He also directed that

Kirsan Ilyumzhinov signing his first presidential decree.

Tanks shelling the Russian Parliament on 4 October 1993.

139

his salary be paid to a local orphanage.

It was not long before Kirsan had, once again, to travel to Moscow where there was a constitutional crisis between Boris Yeltsin and the Russian Parliament. Kirsan went to meet Yeltsin and waited for five hours in Yeltsin's waiting room as he realised that as Yeltsin supported the reforms in Kalmykia, if Yeltsin was overthrown, the Communists could end up back in control in Moscow, and also therefore also in Kalmykia.

After this attempt to meet Yeltsin, Kirsan Ilyumzhinov left in his Lincoln. His driver crashed through a road block whilst a second car carrying his security guards was stopped and the men taken out and beaten. It was a tense time and Kirsan then decided to return to Elista to try to push forward with his reforms as quickly as possible. He also knew that there needed to be some form of economic and political stability. He always believed 'political stability is the milk of economic growth'. There was also the problem of the Chechens whose attempt to declare independence had led to unprecedented fighting and violence so close to Kalmykia. As Kirsan wrote,

> Since the seventeenth century the Kalmyks have linked their fate to Russia. They sacrificed too many lives in the name of the Great Russian state to witness her destruction and ruin with indifference. Someone had to take the first step to stop the fatal process of disintegration, to free ourselves from national egotism, race discrimination and self-admiration. Someone had to embark on the path of self-sacrifice and abandon the great right to self-determination… Russia had given us a lot and now was the time to return our debts.

Boris Yeltsin took more power, and on 21 September 1993 he announced the dissolution of the Russian legislature which in turn announced that it was impeaching Yeltsin and declared Aleksandr Rutskoy as the new president of the Russian Federation. After a constitutional stand-off, Yeltsin sent in the army which surrounded the parliament building. And Kirsan Ilyumzhinov, back in Moscow at the time, managed to negotiate a ceasefire which allowed women and children to evacuate the building ahead of it being attacked on 4 October by the Russian army (see p. 115). Yeltsin then pushed through the fifth Russian constitution, approved by referendum on 12 December which saw him have massively enhanced power.

The spring and summer of 1994 was an invigorating time in Kalmykia. Kirsan Ilyumzhinov pushed through many changes, freeing up the economy of the state, but at the same time anxious to preserve some of the old Communist system which had led to full employment. Initially he had to work through the old framework and it was clear to many that he still had much support in Kalmykia. Then he decided to transform Kalmykia with a new constitution. In the meantime, on 18 October 1994, the first People's Khural of Kalmykia was elected.

With work underway on that, he actively promoted Uralan, the local soccer team, and keenly urged more young people to take up sport. This came at a time when Raimlkul Malakhbekov from Kalmykia became prominent on the boxing scene. And to encourage a sense of Kalmyk identity, the Jangariad was held – initially every year then every two years. This promoted Kalmyk sports including wrestling – there were three categories: elephant, wild boar and lion. Archery, javelin throwing and lassoing of animals brought back to prominence many of the activities which had formed so much of a part of Kalmyk history. And to help try to work with what became known as the 'deportation complex' in which many Kalmyks, especially older ones, remained traumatised by the events of December 1943. This saw a train in 1993 taking some Kalmyk families in a train along the route of the deportation so that they could pay their respects to relatives and friends who died in the journey,

Patriarch Alexis II in Elista with Kirsan Ilyumzhinov.

The rebirth of Kalmyk culture: A mask at the museum of the Buddhist Temple #, boys from School No 3 #; children at the Kalmyk Lyceum #; girls playing Kalmyk music #; and wrestling.

Above: The Lyceum (formerly School No 3) in Elista. It teaches the Kalmyk language to its students and children from other schools. As well as the language, Kalmyk culture is preserved with children actively involved in tracing their family trees. #

The Geden Sheddup Choikorling Monastery in 2011. #

The pagoda in the main square, Lenin Square, outside Government House, Elista.#.

and whose bodies had to be dumped on the side of the rail line. There were subsequent journeys made in 1998, 1999 and 2001.

The Steppe Code

On 5 April 1995 – incidentally Kirsan Ilyumzhinov's thirty-third birthday – he introduced the new constitution – the Steppe Code. Some of the articles were similar to those he had introduced by decree but there was one clause which was dramatically different to the previous state constitution. This clause removed the right of Kalmykia to secede from the Russian Federation. By this time the war in Chechnya, only two hour's drive from Elista, had seen the local government there trying to secede and the result saw the beautiful city of Grozny destroyed and thousands of people killed, and tens of thousands losing their houses. Kirsan Ilyumzhinov and his advisors were keen that this should never happen to Kalmykia. Although some Kalmyks yearned for the possibility of independence, most also realised that this might lead to war and were keen on the close alliance that Kirsan was establishing with the Russian government.

The reaction to the new constitution was unexpected on

Inside the Geden Sheddup Choikorling Monastery in 2011. #

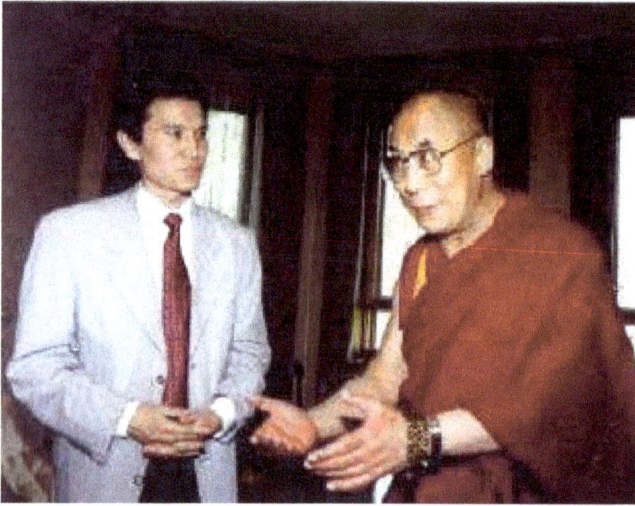

Kirsan Ilyumzhinov with the Dalai Lama.

another level. It was not long before Government House in Elista was fielding telephone calls from luminaries around the world including former US President Richard Nixon, anxious to find out about the new constitution. With unemployment and crimes rates falling, amid trouble all over Russia, the local and foreign press were keen on a 'good news' story from the former Soviet Union.

With his critics claiming that Kirsan was acting without popular support, he called elections early. Held on 15 October 1995, these new elections were essentially a referendum on his rule. He easily won a seven year term, and was re-elected again in 2002. The office of the president was subsequently transformed by the Russian government from an elected position to an appointed one.

Kirsan Ilyumzhinov continued his changes in Kalmykia. Some of these were symbolic. A Buddhist shrine with prayer wheels was built outside Government House in Elista, and the statue of Lenin was moved. The founder of the Soviet Union who had a Kalmyk grandmother, no longer had his back to Government House, but stares towards the building, and also the shrine at the other end of the square. Statues were erected all around Elista celebrating aspects of Kalmykian history. Indeed the Lonely Planet Guide to Russia which first included Elista in its 2009 edition noted that it had 'possibly the world's highest density of street sculpture'.

Freedom of worship had been enshrined in the Steppe Code and there was a resurgence of Buddhism in the country. The Geden Sheddup Choikorling Monastery ('A Holy Abode for Theory and Practice of the School of Gelugpa') was opened on 5 October 1996 – the first Tibetan Buddhist monastery to be built in Kalmykia since the Russian Civil War. Having been constructed on a site chosen by the Dalai Lama in 1991, in spite of it being near Arshan village, some way from Elista, some 30,000 people came to witness the event including several Orthodox clergy. The revival of Buddhism continued and in 1999 the Stupa of Enlightenment became the first stupa built in Elista since World War I. It was designed by V Gilyandikov.

Then an old factory in Elista which had been making building materials, was demolished and in its place a massive

146

The Burkhan Bakshin Altan Sume in 2009. #

Buddhist temple was built. Known as the Burkhan Bakshin Altan Sume ('The Golden Abode of the Buddha Shakyamuni'), and proudly proclaimed to be the biggest Buddhist Temple in Europe – and indeed one of the biggest outside Asia – the temple was on a site chosen by the Dalai Lama during a visit to Elista in 1998. Indeed the Dalai Lama returned to the site on 30 November 2004, and opened on 27 December 2005, it was given its name by the Dalai Lama on 11 March 2006. He worshipped at the temple in an event that brought much prominence to Buddhism in Kalmykia.

Kalmykia certainly prospered during the presidency of Kirsan Ilyumzhinov. The emergence of the free enterprise system did result in much more prosperity for most of the citizens of the new Russian Federation. Business was attracted to invest in Kalmykia on account of his tax laws which made it essentially the 'Delaware of Russia'.

Although there was a revival of Buddhism, Kirsan was

Kirsan Ilyumzhinov
THE PRESIDENT'S CROWN OF THORNS

Izvestia Kalmykia, the main newspaper in Kalmykia since 1918.#

ХАЛЬМГ ҮНН

Kirsan Ilyumzhinov in Kalmykia during the first term of his presidency.

Kirsan Ilyumzhinov unveiling the memorial to the deportation, 29 December 1996.

The Cathedral of Our Lady of Kazan in 2009. #

keen that all religions should be respected. The Cathedral of Our Lady of Kazan, the main Russian Orthodox place of worship in Elista, was renovated. And the Church of the Holy Cross was opened on 19 June 1995. Later a small Catholic church was built in the southeast of the city.

And there was also increasing prominence given to Kalmykia which started to have visitors from near and far. Always keen on chess, Kirsan Ilyumzhinov had introduced chess as a compulsory subject in primary schools in Kalmykia. This programme was overseen by Badma Salayev who served as Kalmykian Minister of Education for many years, and also Aleksey Orlov who was to succeed Kirsan Ilyumzhinov as President of Kalmykia.

President of the International Chess Federation

As mentioned earlier, Kirsan Ilyumzhinov had long been interested in chess. In 1993, Elista had hosted the All-Russia Chess Tournament which was won by Garry Kasparov who ended the event with a simultaneous chess display. This was so successful that it was decided that the International Chess Federation (FIDE) would hold its Olympiad in Elista.

The General Assembly of FIDE was scheduled for 22–24 November 1995 and Kirsan Ilyumzhinov headed to Paris in order to brief the delegates on the progress in Elista for the holding of the 33rd Chess Olympiad. On the first day of the assembly, Florencio Campomanes from the Philippines, who had been the president of FIDE from 1982 announced that, aged 69, he wanted to retire. 'Campo', as he was popularly known, had started as president at a time when chess was very popular around the world but in the late 1980s it was beginning to experience a decline as the watching of videos and the playing of computer games started to gain widespread popularity. Thus in 1995, FIDE was heading towards bankruptcy.

During the presidency of Campomanes, many third world countries had joined FIDE which previously had been dominated by the chess federations of European and American countries. The resignation came as a great surprise and Mohammed Ghobash of the United Arab Emirates Chess Federation, and Bachar Koualty, a Franco-Syrian chess player, emerged as the two possible candidates to replace Campomanes. Kirsan Ilyumzhinov admits in his memoirs that he did not expect the

Florencio Campomanes

150

retirement of Campomanes (pictured left) to take place so soon, but it was not long before it became clear that he might be a candidate for the position. Kirsan was philosophical:

Florencio Campomanes and Kirsan Ilyumzhinov playing chess on the Steppes.

> Political battles and the struggle for power in the chess world are one and the same. And as a politician with considerable power I could serve chess well, since the President of Kalmykia has greater means at his disposal than, say, a mayor or even a minister.

Finally Kirsan was persuaded, probably largely by Campomanes himself, to stand for the presidency of FIDE. Kirsan knew that by being president of FIDE, it could help focus much attention on Kalmykia, especially with the Olympiad being held there in three years. He was duly elected with the support of Campomanes and many third world chess federations.

In running Kalmykia, Kirsan had run into a large number of vested interests from the era of the Soviet Union. These had been intent on frustrating his reforms, and they had failed. However the fractures in Kalmykia were nothing to the divisions in the world chess 'family'. In 1993, two years before Kirsan had been elected as FIDE President, the then world chess champion Garry Kasparov had been engaged in a dispute with FIDE and he had set up his rival Professional Chess Association (PCA) with support from some British and American players. The result was that there were two world chess champions – Anatoly Karpov for FIDE and Garry Kasparov for the PCA. Both wanted to keep their title and neither would play each other as this would result in one of them no longer being the world chess champion. These divisions had reduced sponsorship which had always been vital

151

Gregory Omuku, Kirsan Ilyumzhinov, Florencio Campomanes and Georgios Makropolous.

to finance chess competitions. Some would-be sponsors were genuinely confused, and others felt that they should not become involved in the battle in the chess world. This had all contributed to the dreadful financial state of FIDE.

Kirsan always hoped that a Kalmykian chess player would become world champion. He told Chris Hallman, 'Two factors are important here. The first is that the future chess champion is going to be born here. The second is that a Kalmyk is the president of FIDE. FIDE and Kalmykia will get a boost from each other, and this will create an explosion of interest for both.'

Some of the first moves by Kirsan Ilyumzhinov as president of FIDE were much overdue and were not controversial. Although some chess champions were wealthy, or as in the case of Alekhine married wealth, others had lived in humble circumstances. Vasily Smyslov who had been the World Chess Champion from 1957 until 1958, was quickly awarded a pension of $1,000 per month. In the precarious financial situation in Russia, this allowed him to live modestly until his death in 2010, by which time he was also earning some royalties from sales of books.

There was also one other debt that Kirsan felt duty bound to settle. He flew to Budapest and met with Bobby Fischer. Fischer had always been upset about not receiving any royalties from the Russian edition of his book *My 60 Memorable Games*, published when the Soviet Union when it did not accept world copyright agreements. The royalties had they been paid would have amounted to $100,000 and Kirsan settled with Fischer, paying the debt himself. Fischer cried and said, 'For the first time in my life I haven't been deceived, I've been paid for my efforts.'

152

The flags of Kalmykia, Russia and FIDE above Government House in Elista.#

The 1972 Spassky-Fischer competition and the 1978 Karpov-Korchnoi encounter had captivated world attention but by contrast subsequent world chess championships had been lacklustre affairs rarely gaining much newspaper attention or time on the television news. Kirsan hoped to change this in two ways. The first was to reunite the chess 'family' with a 'reunification' competition. The second was to convert the world chess championship into an annual giant mini-match knockout tournament which was expected to gain more media interest. However the reigning champion was not to be seeded but join the competition in the semi-finals.

The result was the finals for the FIDE chess championship which was between Gata Kamsky and Anatoly Karpov, both born in Siberia with the former having become a US citizen in 1991 and playing as an American. There was a plan to hold it in Baghdad, suffering badly from sanctions with Saddam Hussein offering it as a venue to get some attention back to his beleaguered capital. When the United States refused Gata Kamsky permission to visit Iraq, it was decided to host the event in Elista which was starting to prepare for its hosting of the 33rd Chess Olympiad.

Kirsan Ilyumzhinov and Garry Kasparov.

City Chess under construction.

ПЛАН-СХЕМА
ГОРОДА ШАХМАТ

Karpov easily defeated Kamsky and retained the title.

Then, as soon as that championship was over, work began on the next championship to be held in 1998. There was to be prize money totalling $5 million with the first games to be played in Groningen, the Netherlands. It was hoped that the size of the prize money might encourage Kasparov to play, but Kasparov was determined not to participate and maintain the Professional Chess Association.

There was some scepticism over whether or not the initial Groningen tournament to decide on the challenger to Karpov would ever take place, but it went ahead as planned, helped by generous sponsorship from Halzan, a Russian oil and gas company which was also announced in early 1998. Then there was the FIDE Chess Championship. Held in Lausanne, Switzerland, the Karpov-Anand matches attracted a star-studded cast of spectators including Juan Antonio Samaranch, the president of the International Olympic Committee and even the former Soviet leader Mikhail Gorbachev were both in attendance. Karpov, who admitted his scepticism over the competition, expressed his amazement that Samaranch came to the playing hall every day to watch the games. Kirsan was hopeful that chess might become recognised as an Olympic sport.

At around this time Kirsan Ilyumzhinov spoke of his famous meeting with aliens. Whether the story was apocryphal or to focus more attention on Kalmykia on the basis that 'all publicity is good publicity' will continue to be debated.

Elista prepares for the Chess Olympiad

FIDE has many tasks but one of the major ones is to coordinate the Chess Olympiad which has been held regularly – now every two years – since the first one in 1927. There has long been the hope that Chess might become a sport in the summer Olympics but this had never eventuated – although chess was scheduled to be an event in the People's Olympiad which was planned to be held in Barcelona in 1936 as a rival to the Berlin Olympics. The 8th Chess Olympiad was held in Buenos Aires in 1939 as World War II started, with Nazi Germany organising controversial European tournaments in the early 1940s.

The Chess Olympiad was revived in 1950, and it had been held every two years since then. When Kirsan Ilyumzhinov took over the presidency of FIDE, the organisation was preparing for the 1996 Olympiad which was to be held at Yerevan in Armenia. All previous presidents of FIDE had used the organization to help promote chess in their home country. During the presidency of the Dutchman, Dr Alexandre Rueb, The Hague had hosted the 1924 Chess Olympiad, and also the 1948 World Chess Championship preliminary matches. Folke Rogard from Sweden ran FIDE from 1949 until 1970, and this saw many events taking place in Sweden. Then another Dutchman Max Euwe, took over the presidency. Fridrik Olafsson from Iceland soon after the Fischer-Spassky match at Reykjavik; and before he became president, Florencio Campomanes, a Filipino, had overseen the famous 1978 Karpov-Korchnoi encounter at Baguio City, near Manila, with the 1992 Chess Olympiad was held at Manila just before he resigned.

The decision to hold the 33rd Chess Olympiad at Elista was made before Kirsan Ilyumzhinov became the president of FIDE. He was certainly determined to see that it would be a success not just for FIDE, but in particular for his home town, as there would be a greater focus on Kalmykia than it had ever achieved before. This would be the first major world event held in Elista ever, and the people in the city had a little under three years to prepare for it. There needed to be a chess hall for the games, a media centre, and accommodation for the players, arbiters, officials, journalists and supporters.

Unlike sporting Olympics where the cost of building stadiums now runs into billions, for a chess Olympiad there needs to be a central venue, chess boards and pieces, a media area, and then with players from around the world (many of whom either pay their own way or have national organisations paying for them), the need for accommodation. The main problem for Elista was that it had never been a tourist destination – indeed foreigners were not allowed to visit it during the period of the Soviet Union – and as a result there were only two hotels which would obviously be totally unable to cope with the influx of players from 110 teams, and a host of other officials.

This led to Kirsan Ilyumzhinov's vision. It was to build what became known as Chess City (although the locals always call it 'City Chess'), located in the southeast of Elista. It would be a theme park which would not only serve as a place to host the 1998 Chess Olympiad, but the houses around would be, hopefully, sold off to locals like 'Olympic villages' in other countries, with the main venue being used by visiting chess teams and school groups from Russia and overseas. Work only started in April 1997 with Kalmykian and Serbian workmen constructing the main playing hall – designed to resemble a Kalmyk *kibitka*, and the surrounding houses. Originally Kirsan

Ilyumzhinov had hoped that various chess federations would help in the construction of the accommodation for their players – eventually the Russian government was to meet the cost. At the same time, Kirsan and Konstantin Maksimov and produced a history of Kalmykia, *Калмыкия На Рубеже Веков* ('Kalmykia at the turn of the Century').

In an era with few mobile telephones, and with much communication around the world being by telephones or faxes, a large number of student volunteers came to Government House to work throughout the day and night to try to work out who was going to come and who was not. Many brought sleeping bags and spent the nights in spare rooms at Government House so that they could telephone foreign countries at the right times. People who could speak English, French, German, Spanish or other languages, then started telephoning chess federations around the world. The preparations for the Olympiad energised Elista with the locals realising that it would result in more publicity for their city than it had ever achieved to date. In the end some 110 men's teams and 72 women's teams – each team consisting of between four and six players – attended so the work was considerable.

There were obvious worries that the facilities would not be ready in time but the local authorities thought it should be possible. However there were masked attacks on Kirsan Ilyumzhinov by his political opponents both within and outside FIDE. There were certainly complaints from some of the major chess nations. Some members of the British Chess Federation (since 2004 the English Chess Federation) argued that there were human rights issues in Kalmykia, and in Russia in general. But this had not prevented them attending the 31st Chess Olympiad in Moscow in 1994, and they had gone to Buenos Aires in 1978 at a time when the Argentine military were openly abducting and killing thousands of people including some British citizens. Indeed at Buenos Aires, a week before the 23rd Olympiad, the chief organizer and chairman of the organizing committee, Rodolfo Zanlungo, was himself kidnapped.

At the previous Olympiad at Yerevan, Armenia, where players including the captain of the Guernsey team and FIDE delegate had their hotel rooms robbed, and later made veiled accusations that hotel staff might have been involved. The police in Kalmykia, unlike many other parts of Russia, had a reputation for honesty, and were involved in making security arrangements that went smoothly.

Thus although it was quite clear that Elista would be safe

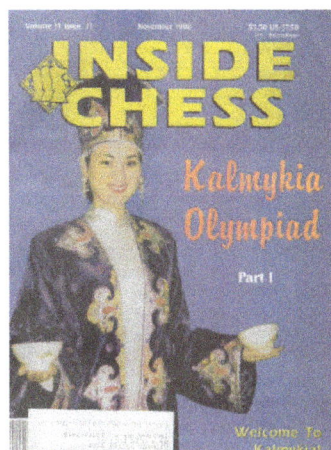

Куда _____

Литва
г. Ничениче

XXXIII шахматная олимпиада в Элисте

Kirsan Ilyumzhinov with the well-known sculptor Ernst Neizvestny and the famous Kalmyk poet Daniel Kugultinov.

From 1993 Soviet stamps overprinted 'Kalmykia' started to appear for sale. These were later followed by a large number of colourful 'stamps' (strictly speaking cindarellas as they have no postal function) on various themes with the name 'Kalmykia' but printed for collectors. A few rare examples exist of them postally cancelled in Kalmykia.

Jean Djorkaeff, the captain of the French national football team and a Kalmyk, with Kirsan Ilyumzhinov, 1998.

The Urulan–2 Youth football team.

City Chess in 2009.

for the players, the concerns remained over whether or not the facilities could be finished on time, and some teams continued complaining for months before the competition itself started. One of the teams which caused much trouble for the organisers of the Elista Olympiad was that from Azerbaijan. They did not have very far to visit Elista, or later to attend the Olympiad but kept on ringing up to check on the building work at Chess City. It soon became clear that the world chess champion Garry Kasparov, who had been born in Azerbaijan, was using the Azerbaijan Chess Federation as a method of attacking FIDE, and Kirsan Ilyumzhinov.

As Kirsan had hoped, there was interest in Chess City and there was an influx of visitors and journalists into Elista in the run-up to the Olympiad. One of the first famous foreign visitors to come to Elista was Chuck Norris. In spite of being a tough martial arts practitioner and actor, Chuck Norris revealed himself in his book, *The Secret Power Within: Zen Solutions*

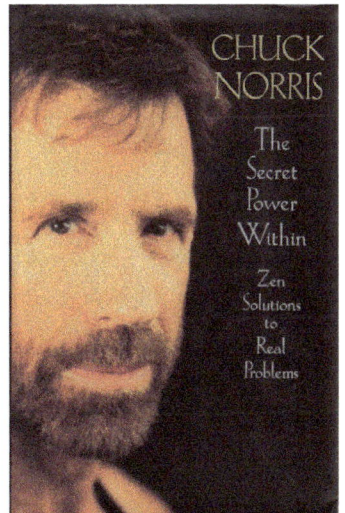

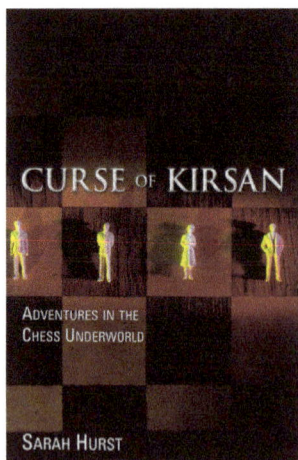

CURSE OF KIRSAN

ADVENTURES IN THE
CHESS UNDERWORLD

SARAH HURST

a bumpy ride through some of the
world's scariest, weirdest places

ABSURDISTAN

Eric Campbell
ABC Correspondent

to Real Problems, as a deeply thoughtful man who long had an interest in Buddhism.

Of the journalists who came, most wrote positively about the 'eccentric' FIDE president, and of his dual role as president of Kalmykia and president of FIDE, with the three flags flying in Elista: that of the Russian Federation, of Kalmykia and of FIDE. There were, however, some critics. Sarah Hurst writing for the journal *New in Chess* went to Elista in May 1998. She visited the site of Chess City and felt that the work was behind schedule. Owing to a severe winter, this was certainly the case. Sarah Hurst did spent quite some time in Elista where she found some locals begrudging the money spent on the construction. In the July 1998 issue of *Chess Monthly*, she was extremely critical of what was happening in Elista.

Another journalist who went to Elista was the Australian Broadcasting Corporation correspondent Eric Campbell. It was not certain what he expected when he was there but Campbell's written account of this trip and his meeting with Kirsan Ilyumzhinov appeared in his book *Absurdistan* (2005), the title alone indicating a somewhat dismissive attitude to the whole region. He certainly sought out some self-styled dissidents, one of whom turned out to be actually a supporter of Kirsan, much to Campbell's embarrassment.

Eric Campbell also met up with Larisa Yudina, an ethnic Russian who ran a newspaper called *Soviet Kalmykia Today*. This paper was printed in Volgograd – long the regional centre for hardline Communists, and indeed the ABC itself was later to report on the resurgence of Communist in that city. Larisa Yudina had been a member of the Communist Party from 1978 until 1991, and as an opponent of Kirsan, she had been trying to collect information on allegations of corruption surrounding the building of the Chess City at Elista. She had regularly criticised Kirsan, and three government officials thought that they could win favour with the president by silencing her. One of them contacted her and offered her some information on corrupt practices. Late one night she went to meet them. Her body was found on the following morning in a small lake near Chess City. She had been stabbed and had skull fractures. The local police quickly arrested the three culprits, one of whom gave evidence against the other two. Understandably there were queries about whether there might be a cover-up, and Russian federal authorities were sent to Elista to investigate. They totally cleared the government of any involvement and all three men were put on trial, found guilty and jailed. Larisa Yudina was posthumously to be awarded the Order of Courage by presidential decree on 10 September 2000.

As a result of the murder, some foreign press and members of a few chess federations called for a boycott of the Elista Olympiad. Most outspoken was Sarah Hurst and also some members of the English Chess Federation and the Australian Grandmaster Ian Rogers. For Kirsan Ilyumzhinov his dream of a chess tournament to show off Kalmykia to the world was now damaged with far-fetched reports being published accusing him of the murder in spite of the Russian federal authorities having found nothing to implicate him, and the killing having been totally against his interests. The call for the boycott of the Chess Olympiad started. Denmark and Norway did not send teams, and Slovakia sent only a women's team. Also missing was the team from Bermuda, hosts of the famous 'Bermuda Party', a social event held at most chess Olympiads, but this was not for any political reasons.

The Elista Chess Olympiad

Finally on 26 September 1998, the opening ceremony for the 33rd Chess Olympiad was held on schedule. As the British chess player Chris Wood wrote, 'once in Elista we all realised that it was absolutely the right decision not to boycott the event. So many people had put so much work into the whole project that the locals would have been devastated if all the chess teams had not turned up.'

Chris Wood wrote:

… on the first night in Elista there was a spectacular opening ceremony in the local football stadium which featured colourful displays and acts from hundreds of child and adult performers. From what was being bandied about on the eve of the Olympiad, I was half expecting to be met on arrival with anti-chess demonstrations or something, but there were no apparent signs of bitterness at all – only a fantastic welcome. I'm not just talking about President Kirsan Ilyumzhinov and his staff, who might conceivable have been involved in some sort of cover-up of dark truths. No, it was the people on the streets that were so genuinely pleased to meet strangers from different cultures. In fact tears were shed by some City Chess helpers when the time came for us all to go home. Most Eastern Europeans never have the opportunity to leave their countries and so, for the Kalmykian people, the Olympiad represents a memorable one-in-a-lifetime experience.

Building delays had meant that the main venue at Chess City had not been completed. The first games were then postponed for one day. There were altogether 634 players, including 171 Grand Masters, 135 International Masters and 58 FIDE Masters. There were also four Russian teams, with Russia C being

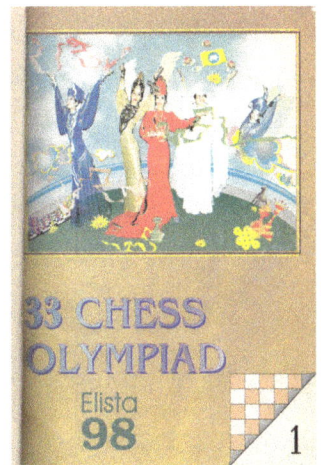

The flags of most of the countries which participated in the 33rd Chess Olympiad.#

A 'cinderella' stamp issued to commemorate the 33rd Chess Olympiad, cancelled in Elista.

Kirsan Ilyumzhinov with the Irish team in Elista.

Round 8: Armenia v. Russia B.

Georgia playing Uzbekistan.

Ruslan Ponomariov (Ukraine, white) v. Rui Wang.

City Chess in 2009.#

from Kalmykia. It was also interesting to note that of the six players in the US team, half had been born in the Soviet Union. Unfortunately the Three Ks (Karpov, Kasparov and Kramnik) did not participate, although Karpov did make a number of appearances. His only complaint was not over the Olympiad but that the next FIDE World Championship would be taking place in the following year at Las Vegas, whereas he had expected it to take place two years after Groningen.

The accommodation at Chess City had been built quickly and the British arbiter Harry Lamb called the housing provided for the participants 'disgusting' and he returned home almost straight away, but most others were too engrossed in chess to worry about the houses around Chess City which were, by all accounts, adequate.

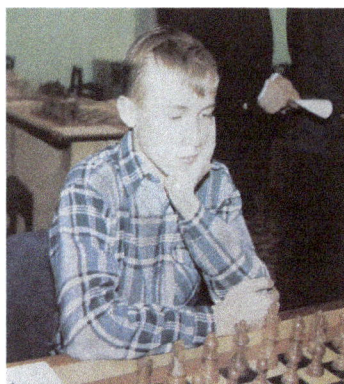

Ruslan Ponomariov, aged 14, from the Ukraine, the youngest player in the Olympiad.

With play delayed for a day, workers continued through the night to finish the main venue at Chess City which was covered in scaffolding, and play started on 28 September. This reduced the days for playing by one with some 2,860 games being played, and only thirteen being declared to have been forfeited. It was to be the first chess Olympiad with the results published online, but the internet site was wrecked by an unknown hacker.

The tournament saw a number of important clashes and, as with all Olympiads, some upsets including one of the top teams from the Netherlands scoring 2–2 against Scotland. On 3 October, the Dutch were crushed when the US team beat them

Ukraine vs USA.

169

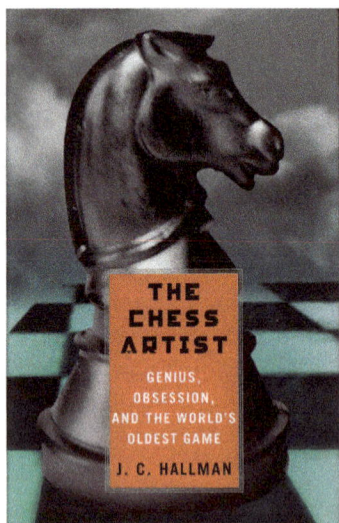

J C Hallman's book, and *Planet Kirsan* by Kirsan Ilyumzhinov.

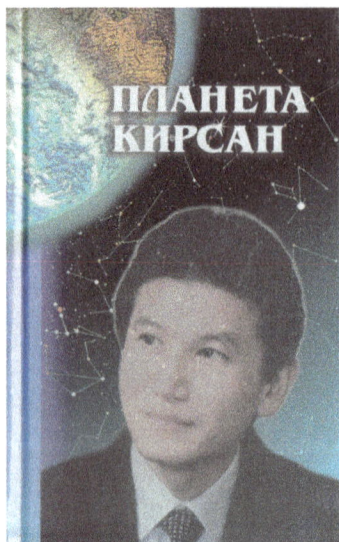

4–0 giving the Americans the lead with Russia 'A' later surging ahead. The US team overtook them again, and then finally Russia 'A' won with 35½ points, the United States having 34½ points, and the Ukraine on 32½ points. The bizarre game played between Tony Miles (England) and Anatoly Vaisser (France) is still talked about as the oddest game ever played at any chess Olympiad. It remains a study in how two impressive players can get tangled up in a game that seems to defy logic !

The Olympiad was a success in so many ways. The people of Elista were thrilled and they turned up in large numbers to watch the games. One elderly man appeared on the scene with a large bed-sheet on which he had drawn a detailed map of the world. Patiently he approached every player and asked them to sign their name in or near their country on the map. Collecting the autographs took up most of the tournament, and when it was all over, he sold the map to the Chess City Museum for $5,000 – a small fortune in Kalmykia at that time. Also at the FIDE Congress, Kirsan Ilyumzhinov was re-elected president, unopposed.

Preservation of the language

It was at this juncture that Kirsan Ilyumzhinov had long wanted to push through legislation to help the Kalmyk language which coincided with the election of the second People's Khural of Kalmykia. From 10–16 May, 1999, an international seminar on minority languages in Russia was held in Elista. Several months later, Kirsan managed to get his Language Bill passed by the Khural, and on 27 October 1999 he signed this into law. A study in that year had shown that some 98% of children entering school could not speak Kalmyk, and Kirsan wanted to preserve the language which would also preserve the culture of the Kalmyks. The act allowed all people living in Kalmykia 'to freely enjoy their mother tongues in various spheres of public life'. With Russian and Kalmyk as the official languages, the law also stated that the government of Kalmykia had a duty 'to guarantee the revival, preservation and development of languages as a most important element of the spiritual heritage of the peoples living in the Republic'. At the same time any discrimination based on the ability to speak, or the inability to speak a language was forbidden – this law coming at a time when some former parts of the Soviet Union, especially the Baltic states, were discriminating against those who could not speak the new official language (which essentially isolated Russian migrants).

Foreign visitors

The Olympiad was certainly the biggest event ever hosted in Kalmykia which became the focus of many television programmes and news stories around the world. For many people in Kalmykia, and in Elista in particular, they began to see more foreign visitors coming to the region. This coincided with greater stability in Russia as a whole with Vladimir Putin becoming prime minister in 1999, and then president in 2000.

J C Hallman went to Kalmykia with a friend, Glenn Umstead, a keen chess player. They were there in late September and October 2000, with Hallman writing about it in the book, *The Chess Artist* (2003). It is thoughtful and reflective, relating how Hallman and a friend went to Elista to play chess. They had mixed experiences and Hallman wrote of Elista:

> All over were the signs of Kirsan's attempts to invigorate the town – new plants here and there, skeletal arch structures meant as support for ivy that had never caught on, new stone statutes standing before buildings cracked and repaired wit alternate shades of cement.

In February 2002, Seamus Murphy's photostory appeared in the *Geographical Magazine*. Focusing on the remote Kalmykian town of Tsagan Aman, it was about the harvesting of caviar in the Volga river. In the following month, Daniel Kalder visited Kalmykia writing about his experiences in *The Lost Cosmonaut* (2006). He and some friends had been to other remote parts of the former Soviet Union, and he was determined to go to Kalmykia. On a superficial level, his book tells more about himself than he does of most of the people whom he met. He complained that there was no McDonalds in Elista, and also fantasized about being sexually assaulted by the local police. However he did include much about the history of Kalmykia which had not been published in English before. A meeting with Kirsan Ilyumzhinov, however, eluded him.

On 23 November 2002, following his re-election as president of Kalmykia, Kirsan Ilyumzhinov once again swore his allegiance to the people of the Republic of Kalmykia. Representatives of the Buddhist faith, the Russian Orthodox Church and Islam were all present and Nikolai Sleptsov, the deputy plenipotentiary of the president of the Russian Federation in the South Federal District then read out the congratulations of Vladimir Putin. Also present were Nikolai Maksiuta, the governor of Volgograd and Anatoly Guzhvin, the governor of Astrakhan, and Garry Kasparov, the former world chess champion.

Another visitor, and totally different to the others was the Australian adventurer Tim Cope. In June 2004 he had left Mongolia to travel on a trek following the same route as Genghis Khan and the Mongols, heading to Europe. Travelling on horseback, and accompanied by his dog Tigon, arrived in Kalmykia in early 2005 where he was greeted by the locals in Elista and found a culture he loved and respected. Later, in the Ukraine, he had to break his journey when his father died, but he resumed it and in September 2007 finally arrived in Hungary. During his journey he filmed himself and his surroundings, with *The Trail of Genghis Khan*, published by the Australian Broadcasting Corporation, being well received around the world.

By this time, Kirsan Ilyumzhinov was spending much of his time travelling around the world to help organise competitions for FIDE. At a FIDE meeting held during the 2002 Olympiad at Bled, Slovenia, Kirsan was reelected unopposed after the Singapore player Ignatius Leong initially announced that he would stand for the presidency, and then withdrew.

At the 2004 Olympiad held at Calvia, Spain, with the media

The Chess Museum at City Chess, holding the collection of Mikhail Taal and a range of other exhibits.#

172

The Dalai Lama arriving at Elista Airport, November 2004.

Tim Cope giving a talk in Geelong, December 2014. #

keen on another chess prodigy, the 13 year-old Magnus Carlsen captured their attention when he became the second youngest grandmaster in history. Quiet and unassuming, but an attacking chess player, he reached the highest chess rating in history.

In November 2004, Elista was again back in the news with the second visit of the Dalai Lama to the city. He was keen to see work on the Burkhan Bakshin Altan Sume ('The Golden Abode of the Buddha Shakyamuni'), and after the election of the third People's Khural of Kalmykia in 2005, the temple was finally completed and opened to great fanfare on 27 December 2005. It was one of Kirsan's proudest achievements with the Dalai Lama returning to worship there on 11 March 2006. Some Russian travel agencies started to offer tours of Kalmykia, a long bus journey from either Astrakhan or Volgograd.

Kirsan v. Kok

In spite of the success of several Olympiads, and an improvement in FIDE's finances, the chess world remained divided and the opponents of Kirsan Ilyumzhinov within FIDE decided to support a Dutch businessman called Bessel Kok in the elections for the president of FIDE which were to be held in June 2006. A chess organiser and the chairman of the World Chess Grandmaster Association from 1985 until 1991, Dr Kok was an accomplished organizer of tournaments and had the support of many chess federations in Western Europe. He promised a higher profile for FIDE, and a lower profile for the president portraying himself as a technocrat.

Rapidly one of the major items of contention was whether

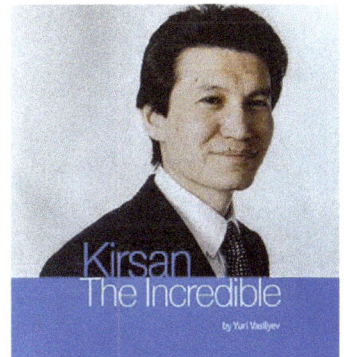

The first biography of Kirsan Ilyumzhinov, published in 2006.

173

Above: The Buddhist temple at Tsagan Aman, 2009.#

Left: Kirsan Ilyumzhinov at another Buddhist Temple, 3 May 2004.

Vladimir Putin and Kirsan Ilyumzhinov, 17 June 2005.

Kirsan Ilyumzhinov presenting His Holiness the Dalai Lama with the Order of the White Lotus Order, Kalmykia's highest civilian honour, at Dharamsala, 10 December 2006.

Bessel Kok could bring any more money into FIDE. He stated that he was keen on getting sponsorship for tournaments and games but did not mention the names of any possible sponsors. By contrast Kirsan had already achieved a strong reputation in injecting much needed funds into chess – many from his own resources.

Each chess federation which is a member of FIDE has one vote, similar to the voting in the general assembly of the United Nations. Thus the Russian Chess Federation and the US Chess Federation have one vote each, as do the chess federations of Monaco and Andorra. Furthermore, there are a number of chess federations representing regions or colonies rather than nation states (eg Bermuda, Faroe Islands, Gibraltar, Jersey, Scotland etc). Both Kirsan and Bessel Kok tried to get support from each of the federations.

By March 2006, with each chess federation having one vote, it was clear from those federations already committed, that Kirsan had nearly twice as many votes as his opponent. However the two slogged it out until the FIDE meeting was held on 2 June 2006 at Turin, Italy, at the same time as the 37th Chess Olympiad. Ignatius Leong had suggested a compromise by which Kirsan and his slate would share positions with Bessel Kok and his slate, but Kok declined as he said that he wanted to change the whole nature of the FIDE leadership. There were veiled attacks on Kirsan and generalised criticism over his wealth. When the FIDE delegates met, Kirsan was re-elected President of FIDE easily defeating Bessel Kok by 96 votes to 54.

The critics of Kirsan had lambasted him – and indeed continue to do so – over the preparations for the Elista Chess Olympiad, but the Turin Olympiad was very nearly a total disaster despite the city having a population some nine times that of Elista and with a vast population living within two hours' drive of the city. Indeed Jacob Aagaard reported from the Turin Olympiad in 2006 in *Chess Monthly* that 'a certain English grandmaster said it was the lowest standard of accommodation he had seen since he first started attending Olympiads in 1982.'

The Reunification Match 2006

As mentioned earlier, in 1993 Garry Kasparov had led a number of top chess players away from FIDE and these had boycotted the World Chess Championships organised by FIDE. Kasparov had styled himself the Classical World Chess Champion, and had held that position until his defeat in 2000 by fellow Russian

Bessel Kok.

L–R: Veselin Topalov, Kirsan Ilyumzhinov, and Vladimir Kramnik in Elista, 2006.

Vladimir Kramnik. With the Bulgarian Grandmaster Veselin Topalov being the FIDE World Chess Champion, many people who had not been following the politics were confused by the two titles.

Since becoming President of FIDE in 1995, Kirsan had wanted to reunify the chess world and fresh from his victory at Turin, he was able to do so bringing Kramnik and Topalov together to complete for a large cash prize. The two headed to Kalmykia to take part in a nail-biting competition that once again saw the chess world focusing on Elista. There were twelve games scheduled with the championship being awarded to the player with the highest score – and a tie-breaker, if needed, to be held later.

The first match held on 23 September 2006 lasted for a gruelling 6½ hours with Topalov eventually blundering. On the following day Kramnik managed his second victory. There was a day for both players to rest, and Kalmykian newspapers of the period show both men visiting various parts of Elista and playing chess with locals. In the third game, Kramnik played very cautiously and this resulted in a draw. Then on the following day there was another draw.

The matches were avidly followed in Elista. Ed Vulliamy, a British journalist writing in *The Guardian* quoted Tambayev Samdjevich, aged 83, a veteran of the battle of Stalingrad, saying that he liked Topalov 'because of his offensive game. Maybe I learned to respect that approach in the Red Army.' Oksana Sitnik told Vulliamy, 'Staging the championship here is the achievement of our President. Kalmykia is a chess nation, and the President reflects that.' And Michail Golsya who teaches chess in Elista was quick to note 'Chess helps to create a rational, conscious sense of citizenship and self.'

So far, the chess competition was receiving scant coverage in the press. This was all about to change. On the day of rest between game four and game five Silvio Danailov, Topalov's manager, complained to the match organisers and also to the press that Kramnik's regular visits to the lavatory were 'strange, if not suspicious'. The world press then became interested, with claims that Kramnik might have had a computer secreted in his lavatory as it was not covered by CCTV. The Appeals Committee rejected the claims that Kramnik had been cheating, stating that the number of his visits had been exaggerated. However they felt that a common lavatory should be used by both players.

With this acrimony, Kramnik refused to play in game five, and it was declared that he had forfeited it. It was later ruled

Kirsan Ilyumzhinov and Michail Golsya watching a chess game, 2009. #

Above and right: Kirsan Ilyumzhinov celebrated on stamps issued by the Republic of Guinea in West Africa, in 2007.

Below: A Kalmykian 'cindarella' stamp.

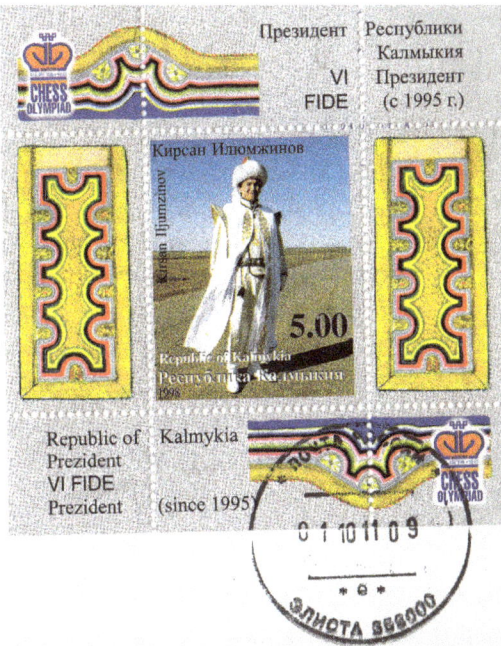

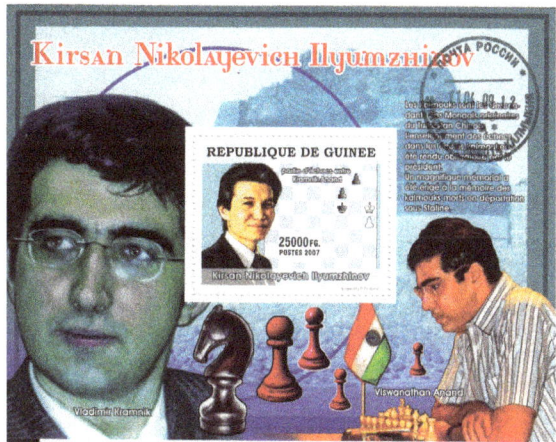

that his team had not lodged their counter complaint before the match as was required by the rules. Kirsan was then called to arbitrate and with matches postponed for three days, eventually the two players met for another draw. Kramnik was in the lead until game eight which saw them level at 4 each. By game 12, the match was tied 6–6. Then there were four rapid tie-break games, a method of playing that was to Kramnik's advantage. He won these 2½–1½, and became the new undisputed world chess champion.

From a chess point-of-view, it was the only series of world chess championship matches where the same opening move (d4) was played in each game. However it was the scandal which was dubbed 'toiletgate' which managed to get much wider press coverage of the competition than would otherwise have been the case. Some later commentators have suggested that Kramnik's actions were not so that he could use a chess computer in lavatory but so that he would upset Topalov's concentration every time he stood up and left the room. As with so many chess tournaments, it was the trivia and the politics that attracted the attention of the press, not the games themselves.

Global Chess
From his dealings with so many chess champions and ex-champions, Kirsan had shown that he was always keen on overcoming personality clashes to ensure that the chess world remained united. He had been aware that there was still some considerable angst in the chess world over his defeat of Bessel Kok, and on 21 December 2006, Kirsan met with Kok in Prague and the two agreed to establish a new chess company, Global Chess BV. Bessel Kok became the chairman and the two served on the board along with Aleksey Orlov.

The next four years were ones of quiet consolidation for Kirsan at FIDE, and also for Kalmykia. Kirsan continued to do his best to encourage chess playing around the world, especially in the third world, with great strides made in China and Vietnam, and large numbers of Chinese players emerged in tournaments during the 2000s. However there was a general decline in the number of players worldwide as many young people continued to focus on computer games, and the internet with DVDs becoming more readily available. Computerised chess games became popular but this soon encouraged a large number of different competitions each having their own system of rating players. Nevertheless, scarcely a month went by without Kirsan visiting another country to talk up chess.

Gradually spending more and more time with FIDE, Kirsan had to hand over more of the administrative day-to-day responsibilities to the Kalmykian vice-president Valery Boyaev who was also, incidentally, a keen chess player and the vice-president of the Russian Chess Federation. In 2008 there was again much press coverage with the introduction of chess boxing, and in the elections to the fourth People's Khural of Kalmykia in that year, the United Russia Party under Anatoly Kozachko winning 17 seats, to the Communists who gained seven seats, with the Agrarian Party of Russia winning the remaining three seats. Although schools, youth groups, and chess clubs from other parts of Russia, the Ukraine, and some parts of Central Asia did visit Chess City, it failed to gain as much interest as Kirsan had hoped. When Geelong Grammar School from Australia visited in 2009, Kirsan did express his hope that there might be a resurgence of interest in Chess City as a venue for chess events as well as other conferences which were also being held there.

Paul Pelliot. #

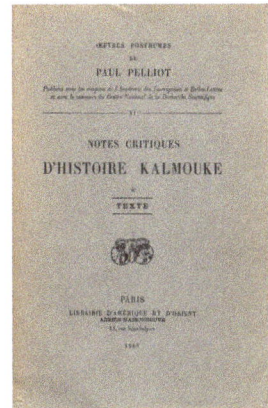

1609–2009

There had been several scholars researching into Kalmyk history in the run-up to the anniversary, in September 2009, of the 400th anniversary of the establishment of relations between the Kalmyk peoples and Russia. The first major work on the Kalmyks in the west was Paul Pelliot's *Notes Critiques d'Histoire Kalmouke*, published in Paris in two volumes in 1960 – the second volume containing extensive genealogies of the leading Kalmyk noble families. Paul Pelliot (1878–1945), a sinologist who had been trapped in the Legation Quarter in Beijing during the Boxer

Kirsan Ilyumzhinov, Valery Bovaev (back centre) and Yelena Pokinanova (front right) with the first western school chess team to visit Kalmykia, at Chess City.

Left: The author on Kalmyk TV.

Below: Greg Toth taking part in the Kalmykia Cup, April 2009.#

The author with Kirsan Ilyumzhinov, 2009.#

The first western school chess team to play in Kalmykia with Kirsan Ilyumzhinov on his birthday, 4 April 2009.
L–R: Mem Arif, Heather Morgan, Alexander Bryant-Clark, Greg Toth, Tim Auret, the author, President Kirsan Ilyumzhnov, Jack Walker (captain), Gary Watson, Tom Claeys, Will Lilkendey.

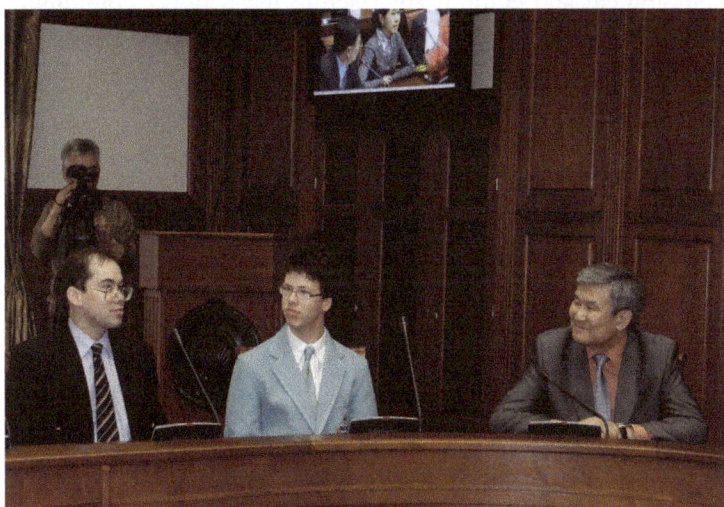

Left: The author and Tim Auret with Valery Bovaev, vice-prime minister of Kalmykia; vice president of the Russian Chess Federation, and president of the Kalmyk Chess Federation.

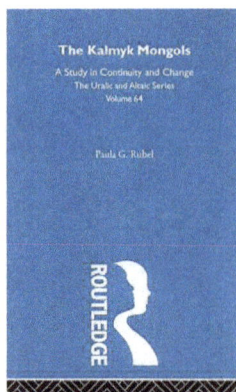

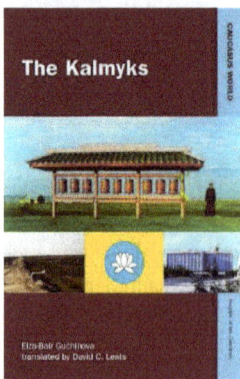

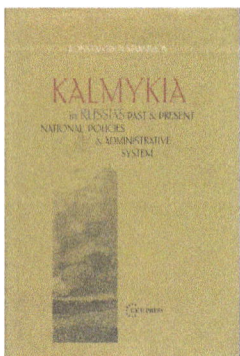

Uprising, had become an expert on Central Asia. Following his death from cancer, many of his papers, including those on the Kalmyks, were published posthumously.

Then there had been the pioneering work of Paula G Rudel, *The Kalmyk Mongols: a study in continuity and change*, which had been published by Indiana University in 1967. This was a detailed sociological study but some criticised the title of the work, but Paula Rudel did point out that was how many of the people whom she had interviewed did identify themselves. In 2001 *The Kalmyk Odyssey* was published in the United States, 'celebrating 50 years of Kalmyks in America 1951–2001'. This included in it names of all the Kalmyks who arrived in the United States in 1951–52.

Elza-Bair Guchinova's seminal work, *The Kalmyks*, was published in London in 2006 and it provided another sociological and cultural approach to the Kalmyk community, and included a large bibliography of works relating to Kalmyks. In the same year, Michael Khodarkovsky's *Where Two Worlds Met: The Russian state and the Kalmyk nomads 1600–1771* was published by Cornell University, providing much information on the formation of the Kalmyk state. And then the major contribution to recording Kalmykia's history in English was Konstantin Maksimov's *Kalmykia in Russia's Past and Present* (Budapest, 2008). Valeriya Gazizova from the University of Oslo worked in Elista in June–July 2008 and completed a Master's Thesis on *Tibetan Studies on Stupas and*

The new Kalmykian history museum, several months prior to its opening in 2009.#

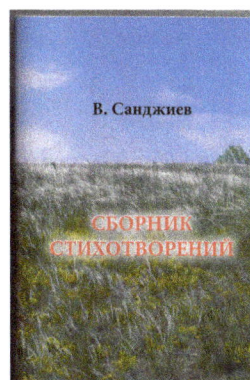

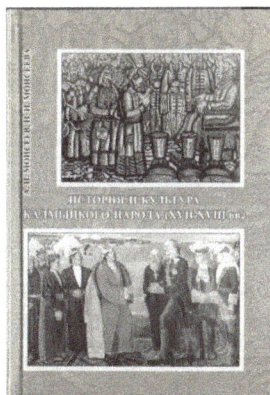

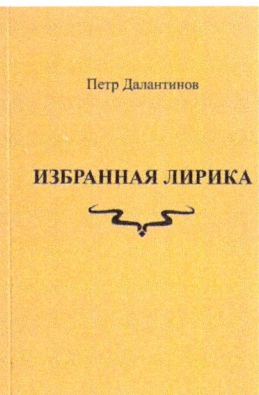
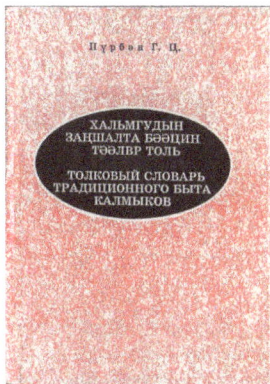

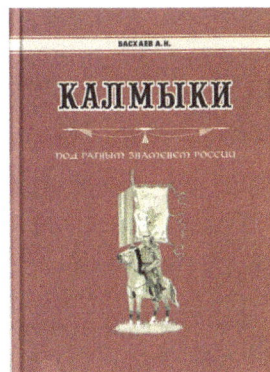

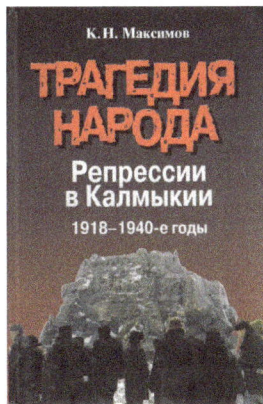
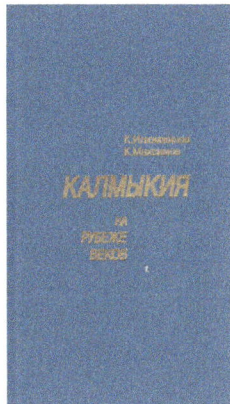

their consecration in contemporary Kalmykia. For the first time, a detailed religious history of the Kalmyks was written in English. Work by Elza Bakaeva continued to detail, in Russian, much about Kalmyk culture. Kalmykia during World War II had already been the subject of Joachim Hoffman's *Deutsche und Kalmyken 1942 bis 1945* (Freiburg, 1974) and his *Die Ostlegionen 1941–1943* (Freiburg, 1976). These books had been followed by Antonio J Munoz's *The East Came West: Muslim, Hundu and Buddhist Volunteers in the German Armed Forces 1941–1945* (New York, 2001), and Alfred Rubbel writing the relevant chapters in *German Tiger Tank Battalion 503 in World War II* (Mechanicsburg, Pennsylvania, 2008). Then there was the massive *Сокровища Культуры Калмыкии.* Printed by the government, this collected together scholarship about Kalmykia and included many photographs which had not previously been published.

There were major celebrations held in Kalmykia in 2009, and the new history museum was opened in Elista. The Russian postal authorities also issued a postage stamp to celebrate the anniversary – only their fifth stamp on a Kalmyk theme (see p. 8). To diversify the tourist industry, the Center for Wild Animals had been established in 2000 where it is possible to see the *Saiga tatarica*, now relatively common in Kalmykia, but rare elsewhere; and there is also a Kalmyk Cultural Village where visitors can ride a horse, camel, and listen to Kalmyk music, and learn about Kalmyk customs.

In the year after the big anniversary, Kirsan Ilyumzhinov declared that 2010 was the 'Year of the Saiga' in Kalmykia. He had already established the Cherny Zemli Nature Reserve,

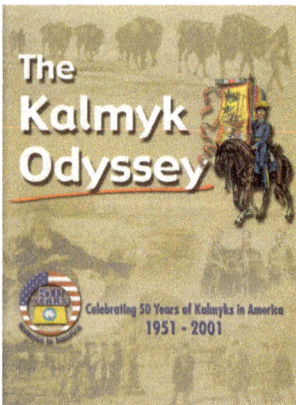

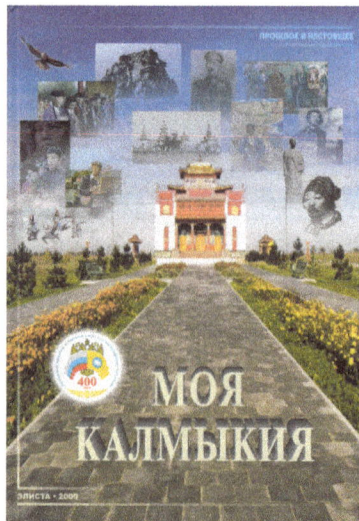

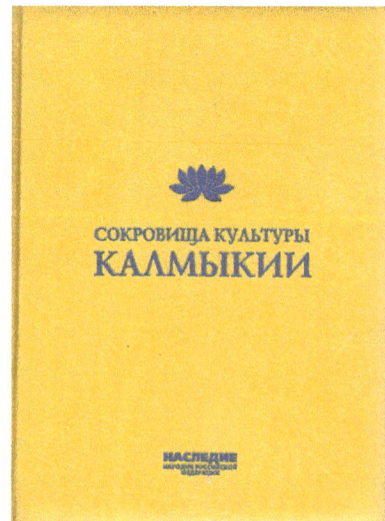

the only reserve in Europe for the strange antelope. Soon afterwards Elista started hosting a number of conferences on wildlife, and many tourists started to travel into the Steppes to see the saiga in its natural habitat. Now extinct in many of its old grazing grounds in China and south-western Mongolia, the saiga population has risen from 21,000 in 2000 to about 81,000 by 2010, although many of the saiga in Kazakhstan were killed in an epidemic in May 2010 resulting in the Kalmykian herds making up most of the world's population of the critically endangered animal.

2010: Kirsan v Karpov

After seventeen years of being president of Kalmykia, and fifteen years of being president of FIDE, in mid–2010 Kirsan had one of the most difficult choices of his life. The Russian government had introduced new regulations which meant that it was not possible to be head of a *Russian* sporting organisation and also hold a political office. Technically Kirsan was not the head of a Russian sporting organisation as he was head of FIDE, but Kirsan was keen that the spirit of the new regulation was observed and this forced him to choose between remaining president of Kalmykia, the land he loved; and FIDE, representing Chess. With a battle looming for the presidency of FIDE, Kirsan finally made his decision.

Kirsan Ilyumzhinov's bid for re-election to the presidency of FIDE in 2010 was to prove to be his biggest political battle so far. Although he had easily defeated Bessel Kok, the four years earlier, this time the US and British chess federations and their allies decided to use Anatoly Karpov to unseat Kirsan. For Kirsan his enemies choosing the former Soviet world chess champion was particularly awkward. As Kirsan had started playing chess competitively at school, Karpov had been his hero, and they were now about to enter what became an extremely bitter election race which culminated in a showdown at Khanty-Mansiysk when the vote was to be held at the same time as the 39th Chess Olympiad.

With all national chess federations having one vote, both sides started collecting the numbers. It was obvious that the US, British and many western European chess federations would support Karpov. Kirsan could rely on a large number of third world countries. Both candidates then started touring the world to drum up support. Because of Karpov's status as former world chess champion, he was able to attract much more publicity to his bid than Bessel Kok had managed to

get. However being a brilliant chess player and being able to run FIDE were two quite different responsibilities and even some of Karpov's admirers thought that he might have trouble keeping together the fractious chess world.

Kirsan was nominated by the chess federations of Russia, Argentina and Mexico, with Karpov nominated by France, Germany and Switzerland. There was a clash over whom the Russian Chess Federation would actually support. With the increasing use of the internet, both sides established websites: www.onefide.com (supporting Kirsan Ilyumzhinov) and www. karpov2010.com (for Karpov). Both asked representatives of chess federations to contact them, and soon both sites started to include flags of countries which supported them, or at least were thought to support them. There were clearly some mixed messages coming from some federations with both sides claiming their vote. As Kirsan Ilyumzhinov managed to get the support of China, Karpov's site claimed the support of the Faroe Islands.

Gradually it was clear that Kirsan was heading for victory, and Karpov, heavily supported by Garry Kasparov became desperate and launched a legal challenge. Karpov's supporters claimed that there were problems with Kirsan's ticket, and that he was using FIDE resources against Karpov. Most of the legal challenges were launched against Beatriz Marinello in the hope of disqualifying her nomination. As any ticket needed at least one woman, her disqualification would be the end of Kirsan's reelection bid. Only just before the voting was about to take place, the Court of Arbitration for Sport, meeting at Lausanne, Switzerland, totally rejected the challenges lodged by Karpov's supporters. The court ruled that Karpov's campaign (Karpov

The opening of the 39th Chess Olympiad at Khanty–Mansiysk.

2010 Inc) did not have the right to launch a challenge, but the individual federations who also launched challenges in support of Karpov did (as they were voting members of FIDE, whereas his campaign team was not).

Then with Kirsan having fended off the legal challenge, after months of campaigning, and millions spent collectively by both sides, the two adversaries faced off in the remote but wealthy town of Khanty-Mansiysk on 29 September. There were procedural moves over countries voting by proxy, and with outcries from Garry Kasparov, the voting then started at 12 noon, and by 2.30 the result had been declared. The final vote was 95–55 – another clear victory for Kirsan and showing that even with the fortune expended in Karpov's bid, he had only managed to garner one vote more than achieved by Bessel Kok in 2006.

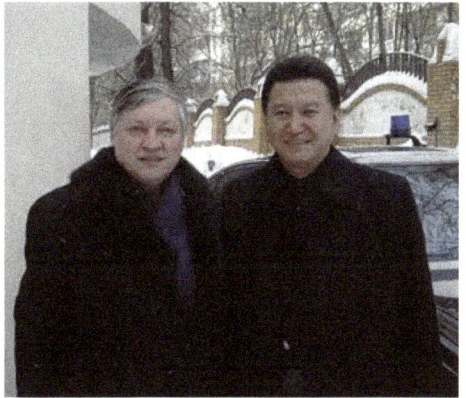

Kirsan Ilyumzhinov and Anatoly Karpov, 12 February 2011.

Winston Churchill always urged: 'in victory, magnanimity', and straight after his defeat of Anatoly Karpov, Kirsan offered the former world champion the vice-presidency of FIDE. As with his defeat of Bessel Kok four years earlier, Kirsan was keen to bring the chess world together.

Chess in the News

Then on 12 June 2011, Kirsan Ilyumzhinov made a surprise appearance on news stations all around the world. In footage released from Tripoli, the beleaguered capital of Libya, Kirsan was playing Muammar Gaddafi at chess. They had met ten years earlier only several years before Libya ended its international isolation and Gaddafi started his regular meetings with Jacques Chirac of France, the British Prime Minister Tony Blair and other western leaders. This time, with war raging in Libya, the meeting from Gaddafi's stance was to prove that rumours of his death were untrue. Kirsan spoke in English which was then translated into Arabic, although Gaddafi can speak English but looked clearly preoccupied, obviously with developments in Libya. And there was certainly speculation in the press that the chess game was cover for a private Russian diplomatic mission to Tripoli.

The chess game itself saw Gaddafi start as white. There are twenty possible first moves, and Gaddafi chose f3, the Barnes Opening named after the British player Thomas Wilson Barnes (1825–1874). The American grandmaster, Edmar Mednis, has argued was the f3 opening is worst possible first move. Kirsan allowed Gaddafi to take back that move (eventually moving his

2011 . 6 . 12

الأخ قائد الثورة يستقبل اليوم رئيس الاتحاد الدولي للشطرنج

عشم الوطن ـ مباشر

2011 - 6 -12

الأخ قائد الثورة يستقبل رئيس الاتحاد الدولي للشطرنج

عشم الوطن

يوني تشطرنج الرئيس الأسبق لجمهورية "كلميكيا" إحدى   01:21

190

Kirsan Ilyumzhinov with Syrian President Bashir Assad.

pawn to f4 – still a weak move), and several others, and was losing the game, although it was declared to be a draw.

Nine months later, on 2 May 2012, Kirsan was again in the news when the Syrian president Bashar al-Assad hosted a three-hour meeting, again set around a chess game, although this was not televised. *The New York Times* openly speculated that the meeting 'reinforced the impression that he is serving as an informal envoy' of the Russian government. Kirsan was able to announce that the Syrian government was planning to introduce chess into the curriculum in elementary schools and reinforce his stance that, as quoted in *The New York Times*, he 'judges leaders above all else on their attitudes toward chess.' Kirsan certainly remarked that Assad was an excellent chess player.

Following his meeting with Assad, Kirsan started investing heavily in a number of countries. He had long been encouraging business ties with Mongolia through his presidency of the Eurasia Foundation, especially the modernising and expanding the Mongolian Railways. Soon afterwards he and the Russian businessman Evgeny Roitman bought a 50% stake in the VIP telecom company which operated in Poland and Ukraine. On 15 June 2012, in Bulgaria, Kirsan's Crédit Méditerranée, registered in Switzerland, purchased some 52.5% of the Bulgarian fuel

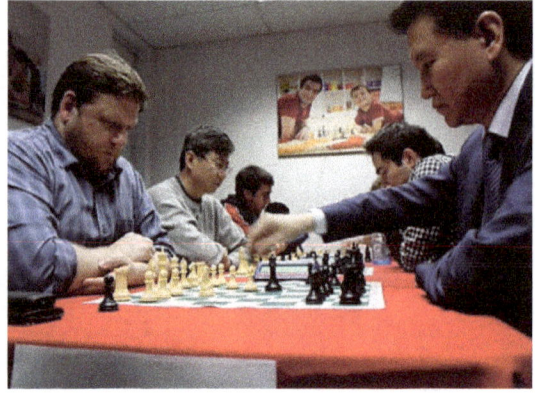

Kirsan Ilyumzhinov at the 12th World Summit of Nobel Peace Laureates, at the University of Illinois at Chicago. Left: With former US President Jimmy Carter; Right: At a local chess club.

Left: With former US President Bill Clinton. Right: With the Dalai Lama, Mikhail Gorbachev, and Songay Lobsang, Prime Minister of the Tibetan government–in–exile. Kirsan Ilyumzhinov and Gorbachev are wearing traditional Kalmykian scarves.

Left: With Polish trade unionist and former Polish president Lech Wałęsa; Right: with Mikhail Gorbachev, Chair of the 12th World Summit.

distributor, Petrol Holdings, with newspapers reporting that this might have cost as much as $100 million. On 13 July Kirsan and the Ashmore Group established a joint investment fund of $10 billion, with an initial capital of $1 billion. Then on 16 July, with Kirsan in Pakistan, it was announced that he had paid between $5.5 billion and $6 billon for Thar Coal, the Pakistan coal company, also announcing that he planned to establish a chess academy in Karachi.

For the chess world, however, competitions continued with the 40th Chess Olympiad in Istanbul going well. There were the usual political problems to resolve. In particular no arbiters were allowed from the German, English, French, Georgian, Swiss, Ukrainian and United States Chess Federations because of their costly court battle against FIDE just before the previous Olympiad which had caused financial problems within FIDE – the losing chess federations not making these good in spite of losing the case. However for the most part, the Olympiad passed off without any problems. The open competition was won by Armenia, with Russia second, and the Ukraine coming third.

The 41st Chess Olympiad was held at Tromsø, Norway. With Norwegian player Magnus Carlsen remaining one of the strongest players in the world, he had been chosen as the official ambassador for the Tromsø Olympiad, and the FIDE delegates at Khanty-Mansiysk had voted to stage it there (over Albena, Bulgaria), by 95 votes to 47. Garry Kasparov challenged Kirsan Ilyumzhinov for the presidency of FIDE. It was a particularly bitter campaign as shown when *The New York Times* on 21 January 2014 published an article headed 'Kasparov Pledged $500,000 to Official in Run for President of Chess Body' which suggested that one delegate had been offered large sums of money to rally up votes against Ilyumzhinov. When the voting took place at Tromsø, the result saw Ilyumzhinov easily re-elected by 110 votes to 61, with Kirsan celebrating 19 years as president of FIDE – a period in which the preeminent world chess organization has flourished, and chess has remained one of the most popular pursuits in the world.

CHESS OLYMPIAD
NORWAY 2014
TROMSØ

Prime Minister Vladimir Putin with Alexsey Orlov, 12 February 2011.

President Dmitry Medvedev with Alexsey Orlov, 1 March 2011.

5.
Aleksey Orlov,
and the continued development
of Kalmykia

On 24 October 2010, Aleksey Orlov was sworn in as the second president of Kalmykia, and the second leader of the state since the end of Communist rule. He had long been a promoter of Kalmykia both within Russia and internationally. He had worked with Kirsan Ilyumzhinov in introducing the policy of compulsory chess in all primary schools, and indeed he had been running Kalmykia's office in Moscow for fifteen years. The western press who generally knew little about Kalmykia wrote of little change in the Kalmykian government. Aleksey Orlov had also been born in Elista some five months before Kirsan Ilyumzhinov. Both had been educated at the same school in Elista, and both had gone to the prestigious Institute of Foreign Affairs in Moscow, with Orlov graduating in 1984 ahead of Kirsan. Both had gone into business, and the two had worked together in FIDE and on many of the major chess events in Kalmykia such as the 1998 Olympiad. However there were major differences in their lives, personality and style of government.

Aleksey Martovich Orlov had been born on 9 October 1961 in Elista, only four years after the return of the Kalmyks from the Exile in Siberia. It was a difficult time for all Kalmyks returning to their homeland with many mixed emotions. Aleksey Orlov's father worked in construction and his mother ran a jewellery shop. As with all those involved in the Deportation, his family had suffered, and as a young boy, his grandmother told him about the experiences of his family during that terrible time. An only child, his parents spent much of their spare time teaching him. He excelled at his primary school both in the classroom, and also with the help of tutors, and from a young age was already fairly fluent in English.

Then he went to School No 3. Each morning as he climbed the five steps into the school, he had to pass the headmistress, Nazedha G. Sergienko, stood sternly at the entrance and watched each student make their way into the school. She remembered every face and ensured that all the boys and girls were well turned out, and punctual.

Many years later teachers spoke of Aleksey Orlov's

N. G. Sergienko. #

195

spectacular school career. He sat at the front of the class and he actively took part in lessons, always raising his hand dutifully. He completed homework diligently. One teacher related that on one day at the start of the term, he had a brilliant performance, coming top of the class. On the following day, he was attentive but quiet. He later queried the mediocre grade he had received for that second lesson. When told that this was because he had taken a far less active part in the class, he replied that he had hoped that he would have gained enough credit from the previous day to carry over to future classes. The one mediocre grade transformed him and thereafter, he was relentless in ensuring that he worked hard every day.

School life during the 1970s consisted not just of the lessons, but also a wide range of activities. The Soviet Union was going through a period of some prosperity, and its achievements were lauded throughout the world, particularly in chess, sports and astronomy. All these were to be important to the teenage Aleksey Orlov. He did play some chess, but did not make it to the school team owing to stiff competition from other boys, including, of course, Kirsan Ilyumzhinov himself who was to become the regional champion. Aleksey Orlov also played tennis, table tennis, football and wrestling – the latter having long been a popular Kalmyk pastime. He enjoyed reading fantasy and science fiction, particularly books by Isaac Asimov.

However Aleksey Orlov's greatest passion was music. Heavily influenced by The Beatles and other groups, he played the drum in the school band which for three years running won inter-school music competitions. There were two school trips to Moscow, and from early on in his schooldays, Aleksey Orlov had set his heart on going to university in the Soviet capital. It would involve moving from a regional town with a population of some 70,000 to the capital of one of the two superpowers, with 4½ million inhabitants.

The teenage Aleksey Orlov's dream finally came true when he was accepted to the Institute of Foreign Affairs in Moscow – the first Kalmyk to attend the prestigious college. It was an event which gained much kudos for his school, with all his teachers and friends knowing that he had achieved it through hard work.

Arriving as a student in Moscow was daunting after leaving Elista. For many tertiary students around the world, their first time studying away from home can be a time to unwind from the rigours of school life. Moscow was also about to host the 22nd Summer Olympics. This had seen a massive building boom in the city and some five million people came to watch the events, some 50% more than when the Olympics had been held at Montreal four years earlier. But for Aleksey Orlov, although he was interested in sports, he knew the real reason for his scholarship. For the first year, he rarely left the Institute. The academic work was very hard and if he was not at a lecture, then he would be found in the library which held some 700,000 books. The school was to train students for diplomacy and international relations, and Aleksey Orlov focused on the study of Malaysia and Indonesia, learning to speak Malay and Indonesian. He was particularly keen to follow the economic development in Indonesia during this period as it was going through a boom under Suharto's New Order. However it was to be many years before he was able to visit that country. And it was not until he had been in the Soviet capital for eighteen months that Aleksey Orlov felt he was far enough ahead in his studies, that he managed to start exploring Moscow in depth.

After completing his studies at the Institute in three years – Kirsan Ilyumzhinov took six years – Aleksey Orlov went into business. He remained in Moscow for a year being chief inspector of Selkhozprodexport, the agency for the export of agricultural products. Then from 1986 to 1989 he was a plumber at the pilot-producing plant Agregat in Moscow. Joining the Ministry of Foreign Affairs (MFA), he became head of the trade union within the MFA, and from 1991 to 1994 worked as director general, and deputy manager of the Russian-Yugoslav Joint Venture Company Sov-Yug in Moscow. This was a time of very dramatic changes in the country with the end of the Soviet Union and the emergence of the new Russian Federation. After decades of the economic certainty of life in the Soviet Union, the country going through a period of rampant inflation, unemployment and hardship for many.

With his company in production in Yugoslavia, Aleksey Orlov was able to travel overseas. It was at this point that he managed to visit Indonesia and found that his knowledge of the language came back to him. He then worked as deputy manager of the Poisk joint stock company, and from February until July 1995 he was director general of the Russian-Italian Joint Venture Company MAG. This was involved in the producing and selling of leather goods, gradually branching out to include Italian shoes.

In May 1995, Kirsan Ilyumzhinov appointed Aleksey Orlov as permanent representative of the Republic of Kalmykia to the president of the Russian Federation, and deputy chair of the Republic of Kalmykia's office in Moscow, a post he held until 2010 when he succeeded Kirsan.

In Moscow, Aleksey Orlov helped to organise the details for many of the visitors who went to see the transformation of Kalmykia. These included Chuck Norris and the German vocal group Boney M. There were also major organisational problems to be overcome with the 33rd Chess Olympiad held in Elista. In the run-up to this, many journalists visited Elista, all coming through Moscow. Paperwork was cumbersome, and there were the regular problems with visas of which all visitors to Russia are familiar.

One of Aleksey Orlov's most complicated tasks involved helping with the visit of the Dalai Lama. Aleksey Orlov, a Buddhist, had long been influenced by the teachings of the Dalai Lama and he related that the Tibetan spiritual leader was not only a 'spiritual leader for all Buddhists, but for me personally a spiritual father'. He saw him as a 'simple monk who brought kindness to so many people'.

In 2010 as Kirsan Ilyumzhinov was about to stand down as president of Kalmykia, there was some disquiet in Kalmykia over the choice of successor. Although there is a requirement that the president of Kalmykia is supposed to be able to speak Kalmyk, there was concern that an outside might be appointed. Thus for many people in Kalmykia there was relief when it was announced that Aleksey Orlov would become the new president. The 39th Chess Olympiad was being held at Khanty-Mansiysk at the time, and both Ilyumzhinov and Orlov were there for the games.

Badma Salayev (right)

Fluent in English, Aleksei Orlov sought to continue Kirsan Ilyumzhinov's legacy of promoting Kalmykia. There were also a number of changes in the state government. Badma Salayev moved from the Ministry of Education to become rector of the Kalmykian State University, being replaced by Ludmilla Ivanova. Vyacheslav Ilyumzhinov became prime minister, and in 2012 Ludmilla Ivanova took that position with Vyacheslav Ilyumzhinov becoming deputy prime minister. Nicholas Ilyumzhinov remained state adviser for veterans' affairs. Subsequently Vyacheslav Ilyumzhinov retired from his government position.

There was a gradual change in emphasis in life in Elista, and indeed in the whole of Kalmykia. There had been hope during the presidency of Kirsan Ilyumzhinov that chess might propel Kalmykia ahead economically. It had created much more focus on the state than it had ever achieved in its history. It had brought in large numbers of foreigners including nearly all the

The refurbished Hall of Sports at the History Museum in Elista.#

famous chess players. But it was now necessary to diversify the economy.

In March 2011 the city hosted a conference on the waterfowl of northern Eurasia which brought together a large number of ornithologists from all over Russia, many European countries and from the United States and from Australia. Elista has also become a destination on the Silk Way Rally, with rally car drivers heading there from Astrakhan on 10 July 2013, and then driving back on the following day.

However with the effects of the Global Financial Crisis, President Orlov has had a hard task but has done much to continue to improve the government infrastructure in Kalmykia. In the area of education, whereas his predecessors had the problem of erecting new school

President Dmitry Medvedev at the Amur–Saman Library in Elista, 1 March 2011.

President Aleksey Orlov with Australian school students visiting Kalmykia, 2013. L–R: Jiga Guichinova, Balsira Elbikova, Alastair Saunders, Matthew Intziadis, Daniel Song, the author, Chris Sreesangkom, President Orlov, Jenny Cooper, Ludmilla Ivanova, Andrew Davey, Gregory Toth, Hashim Hassan, David Raff, Sebastian Saunders.

A year 8 class at the Kalmyk Lyceum, 2013. #

buildings, the emphasis of the Orlov government has been to refurbish and reequip all of them. Within two years of becoming president, students in schools throughout Kalmykia started to see teachers using computers to project information and powerpoint presentations to their classes. The technical logistics of organising this in remote towns and villages was difficult, but Aleksey Orlov was keen to see that the school children could compete with their peers in Moscow and in the West. A few Kalmyk children from the United States have school exchanges in Elista, and there are regular trips by Kalmykian school children to Britain, France and Germany.

Alexsey Orlov with the author, 2013.

In higher education, there has been heavy emphasis on encouraging many foreign students to study in Elista. During the 1960s, 1970s and 1980s, students from around the world attended universities and technical colleges in the Soviet Union. This has continued and currently some 300 students from eighteen overseas countries study at the Kalmyk State University especially in science, technology and agriculture. Some come from Thailand, Sri Lanka and other Buddhist countries, but there have been increasing numbers from Bangladesh and from Africa. And not only have the foreign students benefited, but so too have many local students from learning more about foreign cultures. For most of those who do come to study in Kalmykia, one of the main appeals has been the multicultural society, and the safety of life in the city.

Disused factories and agricultural plants on the outskirts of Elista remind all visitors to the city of the collapse of much of the heavy industry and large parts of the agricultural sector in the early 1990s. This change had happened in parts of Britain and the United States during the 1980s, and came from an increasingly globalised economy. The task of the Orlov government has been to develop and promote new industries. This has seen changes in the lamb and beef industries, in particular with increased emphasis on marbled beef. And the bitter winds that have buffeted the Steppes since time immemorial are now being harnessed with the building of power plants to take advantage of wind power. Two have already been completed, with a wind farm with a planned output of 300 MW is currently under construction in Kalmykia. This has already started to reduce Kalmykia's reliance on fossil fuels.

In late 2012 Kalmykia was back in the world news – and for the first time in recent years, it was not related to chess. On 16 October, the twenty-two year-old Kalmyk kickboxer, Batu S. Khasikov, defeated Mohammed Reza Nazari from Iran

Vladimir Putin's visit to Elista,
16 April 2013.

becoming the world kickboxing champion. Born in Moscow but raised in Elista, Khasikov has also been a member of the Khural (state parliament) since 2008.

However one of the main achievements of Aleksey Orlov has not been in the field of the economy or sports. In a period of tension throughout the whole of the North Caucasus, and with regular terrorist incidents in neighbouring Dagestan and nearby Chechnya, there has not been a single terrorist incident in the Republic of Kalmykia. And indeed it was a Kalmykian, Dmitry Makovkin who had been born in a small rural village in Kalmykia in 1984 who, on 29 December 2013 stopped the suicide bomber outside Volgograd Railway Station. He and sixteen others were killed but Makovkin's actions saved the lives of many others.

Four weeks later, large crowds turned out in Elista on Day 111 of the Torch Relay for the Sochi Winter Olympics as dancers in traditional Kalmyk costumes, and others rugged up against the bitter winter weather, cheered the Olympic Torch which had arrived by train from Stavropol on the previous day where it had been provided with a traditional Buddhist welcome. Batu Khasikov was the first to carry the Olympic flame in Kalmykia. It was then carried through Elista, where Mingiyan Semenov, an Olympic medallist in Greco-Roman wrestling, turned the traditional drum of welcome outside Government House. The youngest of the torchbearers was Dinara Dordzhieva, aged 14. One of the best female teenage chess players in the World, she expressed her hope that Chess might soon become an Olympic

Dinara Dordzhieva (right) playing Chris Sreesangkom from Thailand.

Batu Khasikov (left), and Warren Stevelmans from South Africa, 4 May 2012.

The torch for the Sochi Olympics passing through Elista.

sport. Another of the torchbearers was the local teenager Sergey Konchakov, aged 15, who had helped a taxi driver being assaulted in Stavropol. The torch bearers had been accompanied by horsemen and six horse archers, and the motorcade from Elista left with some 65 torchbearers sharing the route of 14.1 kms east of the city to Yashkul, taking in their wake a herd of wild horses and encountering wild camels at Yashkul.

On 14 September 2014, there were four candidates for the presidency of Kalmykia. The incumbent, Alexsey Orlov, was the candidate of the United Russia Party, with Alexander Boldyrev from Civic Platform, Hongor Marilova from the Greens, Nicholas Nurov from the Communist Party of the Russian Federation and Peter Vyshkvaroka of the Russian Liberal Democratic Party. With a high turnout, Aleysey Orlov won with 80.32% of the vote ensuring continued stability in Kalmykia.

Index

Ingram Content Group UK Ltd.
Milton Keynes UK
UKHW050759130323
418479UK00004B/53

9 781876 586294